Anarcho-Indigenism

T0124472

"Anarchists have much to learn from Indigenous struggles for decolonization. This thought-provoking collection of interviews with Indigenous activists offers insight into points of contact, affinities and tensions."

—Lesley J. Wood, Professor of Sociology,
York University, Toronto

"Combines rich and arresting reflections on anarchism and indigenism with an incisive analysis of the complexities, tensions and affinities of anarchist and Indigenous politics. Vigorously affirming anarchism's plurality, Dupuis-Déri and Pillet also make a powerful case for the reconfiguration of anticolonial struggle."

—Ruth Kinna, Loughborough University
Anarchism Research Group

"Timely, finely-tuned, and establishes anarcho-indigenism as a constellation of personal, political, and theoretical relationships that are crucial for decolonizing Turtle Island and imagining new ways for Indigenous peoples and settlers to live and work together."

—Richard J. F. Day, Associate Professor, Queen's University
and author of *Gramsci Is Dead*

"[A] vital conversation between anarchists and leading Indigenous activists and intellectuals ... who together explore the relationship between anarchist and resurgent Indigenous politics. At its best, this book is an invitation to non-Indigenous anarchists to (re)consider revolutionary politics by taking up the 'political histories and current lived experiences of Indigenous communities seriously'."

—Elaine Coburn, Director of the Centre for Feminist Research,
York University, Toronto

Anarcho-Indigenism

Conversations on Land and Freedom

Gord Hill, Roxanne Dunbar-Ortiz,
Clifton Ariwakehte Nicholas,
Véronique Hébert, Freda Huson and
Toghestiy, J. Kēhaulani Kauanui

Edited by
Francis Dupuis-Déri and Benjamin Pillet

First published as *L'anarcho-indigénisme* by Lux Éditeur, 2019

This edition first published 2023 by Pluto Press
New Wing, Somerset House, Strand, London WC2R 1LA
and Pluto Press, Inc.
1930 Village Center Circle, 3-834, Las Vegas, NV 89134

www.plutobooks.com

Copyright © Lux Éditeur 2019, 2023

Published by special arrangement with Lux Éditeur in conjunction with their
duly appointed agent 2 Seas Literary Agency

The right of the individual contributors to be identified as the authors of this
work has been asserted in accordance with the Copyright, Designs and Patents
Act 1988.

British Library Cataloguing in Publication Data
A catalogue record for this book is available from the British Library

ISBN   978 0 7453 4922 0   Paperback
ISBN   978 0 7453 4924 4   PDF
ISBN   978 0 7453 4923 7   EPUB

This book is printed on paper suitable for recycling and made from fully
managed and sustained forest sources. Logging, pulping and manufacturing
processes are expected to conform to the environmental standards of the
country of origin.

Typeset by Stanford DTP Services, Northampton, England

Simultaneously printed in the United Kingdom and United States of America

Contents

Introduction
A new role: To listen and support

Francis Dupuis-Déri and Benjamin Pillet[1]

Convergences and alliances between anarchists of European origin and Natives have been common in the so-called Americas for more than a century. For instance, there was an alliance between the rebellious *campesinos* led by Emiliano Zapata and the militias of the Liberal Party of Ricardo Flore Magón (who was himself born to a *mestiza* mother and an Indigenous father) during the Mexican revolution of 1910–11; their rally cry was "Land and Freedom." Other examples include the manifesto *The Voice of the Peasant*, released in 1929 in so-called Bolivia by the anarchist activist Luis Cusicanqui, himself a *mestizo* who used the word peasant to also describe the Indigenous workers.[2] As recalled by Ángel J. Cappelletti (1927–95), the Argentinian author of *Anarchism in Latin America*,

the native and also Indigenous masses adopt the anarchist view of the world and society, from Mexico to Argentina [...]. It is seldom noted that the anarchist doctrine of

---

1   Translated by Ellen Warkentin.
2   Silvia Rivera Cusicanqui, "The Ch'ixi Identity of a Mestizo: Regarding an Anarchist Manifesto of 1929," Barry Maxwell and Raymond Craib (eds.), *No Gods, No Masters, No Peripheries: Global Anarchism* (Oakland: PM Press, 2015) pp. 12–21; the manifesto *The Voice of the Peasant* may be read in *Perspectives on Anarchist Theory*, vol. 9, no. 1 (2005).

self-managed collectivism has a close resemblance to the ancient ways of life and organizations of the indigenous peoples of Mexico and Peru.[3]

More recently, the new Zapatistas' uprising of Maya-speaking—Tojolobal Tzeltal, Tzotzil communities in Chiapas, Mexico—on January 1, 1994, was met with great interest from European and North American anarchists who saw connections between Indigenous traditions and struggles and their own philosophies and traditions (see David Graeber's *Fragments of an Anarchist Anthropology*, 2004). Anti-authoritarian and anti-capitalist members of the alter-globalization movement actively answered the calls of the Zapatistas to participate in the 1996 "intergalactic" assembly of "humanity against neolibralism," as well as those coming from the transnational radical network known as People's Global Action and advocating "global action" against the World Trade Organization International Monetary Fund, the World Bank, and G8 summits and meetings.

In the meantime, up north in Canada, Gerald Taiaiake Alfred, a Kanyen'kehà:ka (Mohawk) activist and political scientist, coined the term "anarcho-indigenism," initially in his book *Wasáse: Indigenous Pathways of Action and Freedom* (2005). He then explained that

there are [...] important strategic commonalities between indigenous and anarchist ways of seeing and being in the world: a rejection of alliances with legalized systems of oppression, non-participation in the institutions that structure the colonial relationship, and a belief in bringing about change through direct action, physical resistance, and

---

3 Ángel J. Cappelletti, *Anarchism in Latin America* (Oakland: AK Press, 2017), p. 9.

confrontation with the state power. It is on this last point that connections have already been made between Onkwehonwe [original people] groups and non-indigenous activist groups, especially in collaborations between anarchists and Onkwehonwe in the anti-globalization movement.[4]

This idea was further developed collectively in 2009 during conferences at the University of Victoria in so-called British Columbia, through dialogue between Indigenous and non-Indigenous intellectuals including Glen Coulthard, Leanne Simpson, Erica M. Lagalisse, Richard Day, Alex Khasnabish, Jackie Lasky, and Adam Gary Lewis, and soon after in a special edition of the journal *Affinities* in 2011.[5]

This collective endeavor is part of a more general movement seeking to grasp anarchism, or anarchy, outside of Eurocentric histories and experiences. Among others, valuable contributions to this discussion can be found in numerous studies on anarchist migration flows around the world (such as those regarding Italian and Jewish settlement in the Americas), as well as in Maia Ramnath's *Decolonizing Anarchism: An Antiauthoritarian History of India's Liberation Struggle* (2012), Barry Maxwell and Raymond Craib's *No Gods, No Masters, No Peripheries: Global Anarchism* (2015), Erica Lagalisse's mind-blowing *Occult Features of Anarchism: With Attention to the Conspiracy of Kings and the Conspiracy of the Peoples* (2018), and *Anarchist Studies'* issue (2020, vol. 28, no. 2) on indigeneity and Latin American anarchism (which places a special emphasis

---

4   Taiaiake Alfred, *Wasáse: Indigenous Pathways of Action and Freedom* (Peterborough: Broadview Press), p. 46.

5   Two excellent texts on the subject are: Jackie Lasky, "Indigenism, Anarchism, Feminism: An Emerging Framework for Exploring Post-Imperial Futures," *Affinities*, vol. 5, no. 1 (2011); and Alex Khasnabish, "Anarch@-Zapatismo: Anti-Capitalism, Anti-Power, and the Insurgent Imagination," *Affinities*, vol. 5, no. 1 (2011).

on early twentieth-century popular struggles in Bolivia and on migration across borders of colonial states). Other recent works on affinities between anarchism and religion (e.g. Laozi[6] or Islam[7]) also bring valuable insights on the topic, as well as those focusing on Middle Eastern and African contexts,[8] among which the Black Rose Anarchist Federation/Rosa Negra Anarchist reader *Black Anarchism* (2016), Kuwasi Balagoon's *A Soldier's Story: Revolutionary Writings by a New Afrikan Anarchist* (2019, 3rd edition), and Marquis Bey's pathbreaking *Anarcho-Blackness: Notes Toward a Black Anarchism* (2023) deserve special mention.

Anarcho-indigenism should not be seen as a fancy, brand-new theory or political trend, but rather as a call to action, aimed particularly at non-Indigenous self-proclaimed anarchists (although it is our belief Indigenous individuals might find some insight in it as well). It is an invitation to take the political histories and current lived experiences of Indigenous communities seriously, from a perspective that includes their political, economic, social, and cultural realities. Anarcho-indigenism is not so much a movement as it is an attempt to bring together the mostly settler anarchist and Indigenous worlds in order to achieve stronger solidarity and an efficient decolonizing praxis.

Anarcho-indigenism can be seen as deepening and broadening connections that began with the superficial cultural appropriation of symbols associated with Indigenous people by European and North American anarchists in the 1970s and even earlier. Anarchist punks in London, New York,

---

6   Aleksandar Stamatov, "The Laozi and Anarchism," *Asian Philosophy*, vol. 24, no. 3 (2014), pp. 260–278.

7   Mohamen Abdou, *Islam and Anarchism: Relationships and Resonances* (New York: Pluto Press, 2023).

8   Renée In der Maur and Jonas Staal (eds.), realized with the Kurdish Women's Movement, *Stateless Democracy* (Utrecht: BAK, 2015).

and elsewhere adopted the Iroquois "mohawk" hairstyle to emphasize their rebellious, unruly, and uncontrollable nature. (It should be noted Indigenous people also participated in the punk movement, as Gord Hill discusses in his interview in this book.) In 1977 in Bologna, Italy, an anti-government, anti-capitalist group called the Metropolitan Indians incited tens of thousands of people to take to the streets. Later, in the 1980s and 1990s, one of the loudest voices of the autonomist movement in Berlin published the books *Feuer und Flamme* (Fire and Flame) and *Glut und Asche* (Ember and Ash) using the pseudonym "Geronimo." An earlier anarchist, the Italian Sante Geronimo Caserio, assassinated French president Sadi Carnot in 1894 (his real first name was likely Ieronimo). Within the French anti-fascist network, action groups working against the Front National either clandestinely or in broad daylight often had very expressive names digging into Indigenous-related lore. One such group, calling themselves SCALP (*Sections carrément anti-Le Pen*), produced pamphlets bearing an image of a bare-chested Indigenous man brandishing a war hammer. Author and activist Gord Hill's *Antifa Comic Book* references SCALP and also celebrates the memory of the "Navajos," an anti-fascist group that took action against the Nazis in Germany during World War II.[9] It goes without saying these references to Indigenous lore have fallen under scrutiny by most anarchists and Indigenous peoples outside Europe in recent years, notably for reasons pertaining to illegitimate cultural appropriation.

Anarcho-indigenism has also taken the form of notable (though imperfect) collaborations between anarchist and Indigenous activists, such as during resistance movements against the Vancouver Winter Olympics (see the interview

---

9   Collective work, *SCALP 1984–1992. Comme un indien métropolitain* (Paris: No Pasaran, 2005); Gord Hill, *The Antifa Comic Book: 100 Years of Fascism and Antifa Movements around the World* (Vancouver: Arsenal Pulp Press, 2018), p. 55.

with Gord Hill) and the 2010 Toronto G20 Summit.[10] Since the first edition of this book was released in French in 2019, anarchist settlers have also joined protests blockading the main Canadian coast-to-coast railroad line in 2020, in solidarity with the Wet'suwet'en struggle against the Coastal GasLink pipeline project (see the interview with Freda Huson and Toghestiy in this book), following solidarity movements in the wake of Standing Rock confrontations (2016) in so-called Dakota against the Energy Transfer Partners pipeline project. Other examples include the Indigenous Anarchist Federation-Federación Anarquista Indígena working "to unite the unique anarchist struggle of Indigenous people in the so-called Americas" as well as the 2022 calls for an "active and combative solidarity with our Mapuche brothers and sisters" by the Chilian Federacion Anarquista, in relation to the Mapuche resistance against military settlements in Wallmapu.[11] Outside of Great Turtle Island, in Aotearoa-New Zealand, the Tamaki Makaurau Anarchists echoed these calls when they declared they "recognize Māori as the mana whenua, and the original inhabitants, of this land known as Aotearoa," who "never ceded sovereignty of this land," "support Māori initiatives," and "work actively to redress the fundamental wrongs of colonialism, imperialism, and white supremacy in all their forms."[12]

A shared history of resistance

Many Indigenous communities have long been sources of inspiration for anarchists, due to their history of opposing

---

10 To find out more: Adam Gary Lewis, *Decolonizing Anarchism: Expanding Anarcha-Indigenism in Theory*, master's thesis in cultural studies, Queen's University, 2012.

11 Federacion Anarquista, "Wallmapu: Solidaridad con las luchas del pueblo Mapuche," *Indymedia Argentina* [web], August 5, 2022 (thanks to Marcos Ancelovici for this reference).

12 See their website: https://tamakimakaurauanarchists.org.nz/.

various forms of domination while living in societies devoid of state power. From the very beginning of the colonization of the Americas, the English, French, Portuguese, and Spanish authorities recognized that Indigenous communities could very well become a source of inspiration for some European settlers and a threat to their hierarchical concepts of law and order. The French colonial authorities saw Indigenous people as *"sans foi, sans roi, sans loi"* (without faith, without king, without law), a derogatory expression that can nevertheless be seen as a precursor to the positive declaration "No Gods, No Masters" used in anarchist circles starting in the nineteenth century and continuing to this day. Written observations of Indigenous communities by colonial travelers, including *coureurs des bois* (wood runners) and missionaries, were a source of concern for the European authorities. For instance, Father Le Jeune, a Jesuit priest living in New France from 1632 to 1639, reported that the "savages had neither political organizations, nor offices, nor dignities, nor any authority, for they only obey their Chief through goodwill toward him."[13] Some 150 years later, after a journey in British colonial North America, John Long wrote:

the Iroquois laugh when you talk to them of obedience to kings; for they cannot reconcile the idea of submission with the dignity of man. Each individual is a sovereign in his own mind; and as he conceives he derives his freedom from the Great Spirit alone, he cannot be induced to acknowledge any other power.[14]

---

13 Cited in: Reuben Gold Thwaites (ed.), *The Jesuit Relations and Allied Documents: Travels and Explorations of the Jesuit Missionaries in New France, 1610–1791* (Cleveland: The Burrows Brothers Co., 1897), p. 231.

14 Cited in: John Long, *The Voyages and Travels of an Indian Interpreter and Trader Describing the Manners and Customs of the North American Indians* (London: Arthur H. Clark Co., 1791), p. 30.

Furthermore, observers reported that many Indigenous communities didn't show any distinction between "mine" and "yours"—that is, no understanding of private property—and that relations between men and women as well as between parents and children were in many cases much freer, more equal, and more flexible than in Europe (as discussed by Wendat historian Georges Sioui in his work *For an Amerindian Autohistory: An Essay on the Foundations of a Social Ethic*).[15]

This can explain, in part, the oft-repeated prohibition of contact between Indigenous populations and the newly arrived colonists from Europe (and to an even greater extent, slaves from Africa), with colonial elites fearing those brave enough to run away to live within Indigenous communities would undermine early efforts at building settler societies. In some cases and more specifically in Central and South America (although the Seminoles are a well-known example in North America), runaway African slaves built actual towns and cities known as Quilombo, where natives and the white poor could also be accepted while "shar(ing) the same rights and duties as anyone else. Decisions were made by village assemblies, in which every adult, man or woman, of every race, could (and most would) participate," as recalled by Pedro Ribeiro in an essay about black anarchism.[16]

Between the sixteenth and eighteenth centuries, Europe went through a series of profound changes that caused the existing system of government to become increasingly author-

---

15   See also Francis Dupuis-Déri, "L'Amérindien philosophe: entrevue avec Georges E. Sioui," *Argument*, vol. 2, no. 2 (2000), www.revueargument.ca/article/2000-03-01/117-lamerindien-philosophe-entrevue-avec-georges-e-sioui.html.

16   Pedro Ribeiro, "Senzala or Quilombo: Reflections on APOC and the Fate of Black Anarchism," *Black Anarchism: A Reader* (Black Rose Anarchist Federation/Rosa Negra Anarchista Federacion, 2016).

itarian, disciplinary, and punitive.[17] State militaries gradually modernized their outreach by mandating forced recruitment as a way to build their royal and colonial military forces, the patriarchy tightened its grip on European women, and the emerging capitalist system went into full bloom by privatizing lands previously held in common through what is now known as the enclosure system. The resulting widespread poverty displaced whole populations, who—among other things— migrated into the cities where they had to turn to wage-based work or were sent abroad as cannon fodder in the budding colonies. Radical dissidents were tortured or assassinated by the state under the pretext of fighting witchcraft or reducing vagrancy.

European colonial authorities feared the defection of their own forces, which they described under the idea of *ensauvagement* ("turning savage" in French), a derogatory term associating Indigenous people to animals and the wilderness. This, of course, was not a new concept, with Enlightenment thinkers building on previous European understandings of human nature. The "savage" was to the New World what the "barbarian" had been to the Ancients: a previous state

---

17   With regard to the use of torture in Europe, see the first page of Michel Foucault, *Discipline and Punish* (New York: Pantheon, 1977) where the author describes the execution of a man named Damiens for regicide.

The flesh was torn with red-hot pincers from his breast, arms, thighs and calves, his right hand burnt with sulphur and, on those places where the flesh will be torn away, poured molten lead, boiling oil, burning resin wax and sulphur melted together, and then his body drawn and quartered by four horses and his limbs and body consumed by fire, reduced to ashes and his ashes thrown to the winds.

Such a description provides a certain perspective vis-à-vis the shock and horror expressed in response to the torture practiced by the so-called "uncivilized" Indigenous peoples on the Jesuit missionaries in New France, who were subsequently given the title of "martyr saints" in the official story of Quebec's history.

of nature, a terrible threat, something to be frightened of, to vanquish, to assimilate or exterminate,[18] but also a mirror, creating the image of a perceived threat to the dominant order to become an attractive promise to those bearing the brunt of it. To "turn savage" meant to emancipate oneself, to have the freedom to form relationships based on liberty, equality, solidarity, and safety, the opposite of the hierarchical and disciplinary European monarchic and aristocratic societies of the time. Historian Richard White reported this anecdote about the French king's officer, Marquis de La Salle, who had left some of his troops at a small fort before going on an expedition. "On his return to Illinois in 1680, La Salle found that his men had not only deserted but had also demolished his fort, stolen his goods, and, in the hand of a man La Salle recognized as Le Parisien, had left scrawled on a board a parting epithet: *Nous sommes touts Sauvages*" ["We are all savages"].[19] Many similar examples of desertion and "return to the wild" can be found in the literature, including by women who found that relations between sexes were much freer, more equal, and more fluid in many Indigenous communities than in Europe. Many European women who were captured by Indigenous people refused to be "liberated" by their fathers, brothers, or former companions.[20]

Although much could be said from a critical perspective about the stereotypical and Eurocentric trope of associating concepts such as "nature," "wilderness," "freedom," and

18   Joëlle Gardette, *Les Innus et les Euro-Canadiens* (Quebec: Presses de l'Université Laval, 2008), pp. 36 and 41. See also: Olive P. Dickason, *The Myth of the Savage* (Edmonton: University of Alberta Press, 1984).

19   Richard White, *The Middle Ground: Indians, Empires and Republics in the Great Lakes Region, 1650–1815* (New York: Cambridge University Press, 1991), p. 105.

20   See Laura F. Klein and Lillian A. Ackerman (eds.), *Women and Power in Native North America* (Norman: University of Oklahoma Press, 1995).

"indigeneity,"[21] the popularity of such connections cannot be denied even among Indigenous people today. Examples include Savage Family, a hip-hop collective from Kansas, founded in 2001, which advocates resistance to colonialism and racism.[22] Taking the notion a step further, Pessamit Innu poet Joséphine Bacon published a poetry collection with José Acquelin entitled *We Are All Savages*, in which some poems refer directly to resistance and destruction:

> we are all savages
> we all deserve the poetic therapy
> that the Earth has set aside for us still
> it's the resistance of the last boars
> against the armada of warrior pigs
> [...]
> we are all savages
> packed in tightly together
> reduced in number by the other
> we are naked and one
> in the same boat
> on the same raft[23]

---

21   Benjamin Pillet, "Die dekoloniale Ökologie und der Diskurs wom Ökologischen Edlen Wilden," in Jana Pinosová, Susanne Hose, and Marcel Langer (eds.), *Minderheit—Macht—Natur: Verhandlungen im Zeitalter des Nationalstaats* (Bautzen: Sorbisches Institut, 2022), pp. 129–145.

22   Julien Gignac, "Meet the Militant Indigenous Rap Group Promoting Extreme Resistance," *Vice*, March 10, 2017 [www.vice.com/en_ca/article/qkm3pb/meet-the-militant-indigenous-rap-group-promoting-extreme-resistance].

23   Free translation from: Joséphine Bacon and José Acquelin, *Nous sommes tous des sauvages* (Montreal: Mémoire d'encrier, 2011), p. 18 (note: José Acquelin titled another of his poetry collections *Anarchie de la lumière* [Anarchy of Light]).

Even more provocatively, An Antane Kapesh, an Innu from Schefferville, Quebec, published her autobiography in 1976 under the title *Je suis une maudite sauvagesse/Eukuan nin matshimanitu innu-iskueu* (I am a Damn Savage).[24] In it, she wrote:

> I am a damn savage. I am very proud when I hear myself called that today. When I hear the White Man say that word, I understand that he is telling me over and over that I am a real Indian, that I was the first to live in the woods. And everything that lives in the woods corresponds to the best life. May the White Man always call me a savage.[25]

However, the dual opposition between "savage" and "civilization" has also met with resistance from anarchist and colonized people. Mohamed Saïl, a Kabyle anarchist born in Algeria at the end of the nineteenth century and active in militant networks in France from the 1920s, strongly criticized Europe's tendency to self-identify as the "heartland of civilization" and to relegate all non-Europeans to the status of savages. In 1926, he published an article in the anarchist paper *L'Insurgé* called "Civilization!" in which he opened with the question: "Who should be given the title of savage? Those who, when they pass, leave behind only ruins and death? Or those who never thought to have to defend themselves from Europeans?"[26] He also suggested that the traditions of the Kabyles, an Algerian Berber ethnic group, were characterized by a "federalist and libertarian temperament" shown by their refusal to be governed by any external powers and by the desire to govern themselves via village councils.[27]

---

24 Published under the name Anne André: *Je suis une maudite sauvagesse— Eukuan Nin Matshimanitu Innu-Iskueu* (Montreal: Leméac, 1976).

25 Free translation from: *Ibid.*, p. 241.

26 Free translation from: Mohamed Saïl, "Civilisation!," *L'Insurgé*, June 26, 1926, no. 60.

27 Free translation from: Mohamed Saïl, "La mentalité kabyle," *Le Libertaire*,

It should be noted the phrase "Indigenous" is mostly used as an umbrella concept that tends to obscure a vast diversity of political and social systems across time and space. Although some precolonial Indigenous societies were indeed more egalitarian than their European counterparts, many were not. In "Anarchism: A Māori perspective," Metiria Turei explained, for instance, that "being Māori, identifying with Mana Māori and believing in the principles of anarchism is a seemingly huge paradox, full of insurmountable contradiction [...] especially as the traditional Māori structure of society is hierarchical, patriarchal, oppressive and sexist" and was "ordered into *rangatira* (ruling class), *tutua* (commoners), and *taurekareka* (slaves)." Yet, she also suggests that the past doesn't determine the future and that "only through cultural growth will Māori society be able to discard the oppressive and hierarchical structures of the past and develop into a free and egalitarian society."[28] In the present book, J. Kēhaulani Kauanui, a diasporic Kanaka Maoli (Native Hawaiian) born in California, also addresses the Hawai'i Indigenous monarchy, thereby reminding us of the differences between the more hierarchical Indigenous systems and the authoritarian hierarchies of Europe, and Roxanne Dunbar-Ortiz, a settler Marxist activist and a scholar specializing in Indigenous history, brings up examples of hierarchical Indigenous social structures in New France. The same caveat can be applied to feminism and gender relations: while women are often at the forefront of anarcho-indigenist thought and action, not all Indigenous peoples share the same history—or the same current under-

---

February 16, 1951.

28 Metiria Turei, "Anarchism: A Māori Perspective," *The Anarchist Library*, originally published in 1993. Note that the author has since been the co-leader of the Green Party, in Aotearoa-New Zeland. See also the website of the Tamaki Makaurau Anarchists.

standing—in this regard (see the interview with Véronique Hébert).

None of the aforementioned precolonial societies and communities were devoid of violence, yet they generally appeared much fairer and more agreeable than any options Europe was proposing at the time to some settlers. As mentioned earlier, some white settler women who had been taken away by Natives refused to come back to the colonial societies when given a chance by settler marshals or troopers, due to the relative freedom and equality they enjoyed in their new life.[29] These societies were therefore used as a reference point for radical critical thought about how hierarchical societies are shaped by domination and oppression. The French Baron of Lahontan, who lived for a period with some Indigenous communities in what was considered at the time the borderlands of New France, offered such a critical perspective in his book *Dialogues avec un sauvage*, published in 1704. Featuring a fictitious wise Indigenous man Adario, inspired by the real-life chief Wendat Kondiaronk, Lahontan tears down one by one the arguments of a European man trying to prove the political, social, and moral superiority of Europe. (This example is also discussed in David Graeber and David Wengrow, *The Dawn of Everything: A New History of Humanity*, 2021.)[30]

Some two hundred years later, the famous Russian anarchist geographer Peter Kropotkin took that same idea and developed it in his book *Mutual Aid: A Factor of Evolution*.[31] At the time, European intellectual elites were debating Darwin's popularized theories of the war of all against all and the "survival of the fittest," while prominent sociologists were attempting

---

29   Susan Faludi, *The Terror Dream: Myth and Misogyny in an Insecure America* (London: Picador, 2008).

30   Lahontan, *Dialogues avec un sauvage* (Montréal: Lux, 2010).

31   Peter Kropotkin, *Mutual Aid: A Factor of Evolution* (London: Heinemann, 1908).

to use those same concepts to justify state domination and capitalistic competition. Conversely, Kropotkin sought to show that natural and human history revealed mutual aid to be a much more significant factor than combat and competition in the survival and development of species and societies. He used references to some Indigenous peoples to support his ideas, arguing that these communities didn't have private property or use coercive leadership, and that they practiced mutual aid and made decisions collectively through village councils. Since then, Kropotkin's argument has been used frequently by anthropologists with anarchist sympathies, including Pierre Clastres in the 1970s, Harold Barclay in the 1990s, and more recently David Graeber and Marshall Sahlins, as well as political scientist James C. Scott. Sociologist and philosopher John Holloway drew on the contemporary experience of the Zapatistas to propose the idea of "changing the world without taking power."[32]

New social movements of the 1960s and 1970s

Yet, while the notion of anarcho-indigenism as formulated in the early 2000s in so-called Canada can be read in continuity with radical understandings of power in the colonial fringes

---

32   Guilherme Lavinas Jardim Falleiros, "From Proudhon to Lévi-Strauss and Beyond: A Dialogue between Anarchism and Indigenous America," *Anarchist Studies*, vol. 26, no. 2 (2018); Pierre Clastres, *La société contre l'État* (Paris: Minuit, 1974); Pierre Clastres, "La question du pouvoir dans les sociétés primitives," *Interrogations*, no. 7 (1976); Harold Barclay, *People without Government: An Anthropology of Anarchy* (London: Kahn & Averill, 1990); Marshall Sahlins, *The Western Illusion of Human Nature* (Chicago: Prickly Paradigm Press, 2008); David Graeber, *Fragments of an Anarchist Anthropology* (Chicago: Prickly Paradigm Press, 2004); David Graeber, *The Democracy Project: A History, a Crisis, a Movement* (New York: Spiegel & Grau, 2013); James C. Scott, *The Art of Not Being Governed* (New Haven: Yale University Press, 2009); John Holloway, *Change the World Without Taking Power* (New York: Pluto Press, 2003). See also Amartya Sen, *La démocratie des autres* (Paris: Payot-Rivages, 2005).

of Europe since the sixteenth century, it is also informed by the social changes that have taken place globally since the 1950s and 1960s. The end of World War II brought with it a paradigm shift both for anarchism and Indigenous peoples. Anarchist movements had been greatly weakened by the conflict, targeted as they were by fascist and Stalinist totalitarianism. In the Americas, many Indigenous soldiers returned from the war only to be denied any form of official recognition for their sacrifices on the battlefields of Europe—a homecoming similar to that experienced by combatants from British and French colonies in Africa and Asia (see the interview with Clifton Ariwakehte Nicholas). For these young veterans, their participation in the liberation of Europe deserved more than a simple handshake or medal, particularly after helping European people fight against the same imperialistic evils they had imposed (and continued to) upon them. They had liberated Europe; surely they'd be able to liberate themselves next? The consequent revival of the struggle for national liberation would result in the formal (if somewhat less than genuine) decolonization of most territories under European control.

Many intellectual and political ties exist between advocates of decolonization and the European communist parties. While this relationship may have been at times a source of conflict, and while the communist commitment to decolonization has often been called into question by colonized peoples, the current conversation surrounding decolonization has nonetheless been influenced in the long term by a vocabulary and a set of theoretical models inherited from Marxism, which is closely tied to anarchism (see the interview with Roxanne Dunbar-Ortiz). The anti-colonial rhetoric of the 1960s and 1970s was focused on issues of language and culture, but also on a rejection of the imperialist agenda and a consideration of social class. The Marxist influence spread throughout North America, where echoes were heard in African American organizations such as the Black Panther Party as well as in the Indigenous Red Power movement, with such advocates as Howard Adams and Leonard Peltier. Similarly, African American and Indigenous groups were often inspired by the same intellectuals and activists, including Frantz Fanon, Malcolm X, and Kwame Nkrumah, who promoted ideas about Third World nationalism, anti-racism and anti-capitalism. However, it must be stated that the left-leaning element of the decolonization movement is often criticized by African American and Indigenous activists who see in it two inherent risks: first, the risk of seeing the anti-colonial struggle exploited by predominantly white leftist parties and organizations looking to attract new partisans; and second, the members of these same leftist parties often seeming keen to fight the class war but remaining relatively quiet about the very real struggles in the daily life of a person of color.

Resistance to the Vietnam War and the emergence of the New Left only confirmed the concerns of Indigenous activists. At the time, leftist criticism of Soviet totalitarianism gradually widened the existing rift between the extreme libertarian left and orthodox Marxism. Hope that the movement would bring about an actual revolution gradually withered and was replaced among the Marxist left by plans for slow, progressive political reformation. Meanwhile, the New Left endeavored to create real utopias and establish a form of political engagement that was formerly only deemed possible after the revolution: the idea of being able to live according to one's anti-authoritarian and anarchist principles on a daily basis. The rejection of hierarchy and authority therefore became a subject of heated debate among leftists, creating a momentum that eventually culminated in the hippie, pacifist, anti-nuclear, radical feminist and Afro-American movements (among others).

Another interesting dynamic that emerged in the 1960s was the consolidation of ecologist movements, which began using cooperative and participative strategies and anti-hierarchical grassroots structures previously associated with anarchism. Peter Marshall boldly labels the evolution of "green" anarchism and primitivism as one of the major developments of "second wave" anarchism.[33] This, in turn, led to a new relationship between anti-authoritarian anarchist activists and Indigenous peoples. It also prompted the re-emergence of stereotypes, not unlike those of the late nineteenth century, presenting Indigenous peoples as the last noble survivors of savage populations, incompatible with capitalist progress and therefore doomed to disappear,[34] something that can be widely found in primitivist literature.

The re-emergence of these tropes can be explained by two main factors. Firstly, North American popular culture, largely shaped by cinematic and dime-store novel images of the Far West, had long been presenting a simplified version of the colonial dichotomy in the form of the cowboy-versus-Indian narrative. It is therefore unsurprising that advocacy movements seeking symbols and leaders to draw people together would want to identify with such national antiheroes.[35] The second factor is related to the ecologist movements themselves. Starting in the 1960s, the ecologist ideal—conceptualized as being close to nature—became increasingly associated with Indigenous figures (although the connection had already been made by early proponents of conservationism). Take, for example, the approximate quotation from a

---

33   The first wave ("classical" anarchism) is based on proletarian values and closely linked to Marxist analyses and theories (Peter Marshall, *Demanding the Impossible: A History of Anarchism* (Oakland: PM Press, 2010)).

34   These stereotypes are based on European Enlightenment concepts dating back to the beginning of the American colonization project and inspired by Jean-Jacques Rousseau's "noble savage."

35   This is hardly a recent phenomenon—think back to the Apache subculture in Paris during La Belle Époque.

speech allegedly given by an Indigenous chief named Seattle (a speech which came to epitomize modern American environmental beliefs), which began to circulate widely, or the memorable "Keep America Beautiful" television advert featuring the actor Iron Eyes Cody.[36] These stereotypes of the "noble savage environmentalist" figured prominently in the anarcho-primitivist or green anarchist movements promoted by John Zerzan, Derrick Jensen, and the Earth First! organization (see comments by Roxanne Dunbar-Ortiz on the subject of anti-civilization anarchism).

While connections were being made between anarchism and Indigenous peoples in the 1960s, these new ties were, once again, mainly one-sided and somewhat exploitative. Anarchists were finding a source of inspiration and a justification for their ideology in stereotypical Indigenous peoples, while simultaneously reducing them to essentialist tropes that only rarely escaped the museum-case status in which western societies still tend to enclose them. The relationship was a continuation of the same old ethnographic analysis that, even in books by anarchists like Kropotkin, had a hard time breaking away from modernist, linear teleology based on exclusive binaries such as "civilization versus wilderness" or "progress versus primitivism." But while the anarchists of the nineteenth century appropriated these binaries and used them to argue against the era's popular theories of Social Darwinism, the green anarchists of the twentieth century attempted to associate themselves with one of these terms (wilderness, primitivism) in the hopes of opposing the other (civilization, progress).

36　We should note here that Iron Eyes Cody (born Espera Oscar de Corti) is one of many non-Indigenous public figures who have claimed Indigenous identity for reasons that may be related to environmental principles (including also Grey Owl—born Archibald Belaney—and Joseph Boyden, both Canadian citizens from strictly European descent).

The 1980s and 1990s

Outside of the occasional interest of a few individual anarchists in the Indigenous cause, however, Indigenous people largely remained at the margins of the anarchist movement until at least the 1990s. It could be argued the shift originated in Central America—although the movement later called "Indigenism," which gradually took hold in international bodies such as the United Nations,[37] and nationwide Indigenous movements in the wake of the new Canadian Constitution in the early 1980s (among other examples) would tend to suggest this paradigm shift happened on a global scale. Faced with neoliberal regimes supported by Reagan's America, the Central American left was able to organize and build new alliances between the mainly urban Marxist left and the rural populations, which were predominantly Indigenous.

This phenomenon was particularly evident in Mexico, where neoliberal reforms led to the 1989 coffee crisis, pushing the Marxist-Leninist farmers' organizations, composed mainly of Indigenous *campesinos*, to shift their ideological stance. As the world became increasingly sympathetic to the Indigenous perspective, spurred by progressive representation at the United Nations by the American Indian Movement and other Indigenous movements outside of the Americas, Mexican farmers' organizations began to place emphasis on their indigeneity to bring legitimacy to their active resistance. This phenomenon culminated in the Zapatista uprising and its aftermath.

The reappropriation of Indigenous themes by the Zapatista movement did not go unnoticed. Indeed, it resonated in extreme-left circles, which saw it as an excellent example of resistance against neoliberalism. In the Americas, 1992 was a year punctuated by 500th anniversary celebrations of the "dis-

---

37 Ronald Niezen, *The Origins of Indigenism: Human Rights and the Politics of Identity* (Berkeley: University of California Press, 2003).

covery" of the continent. These were strongly contested by Indigenous grassroots organizations, which staged their own counteractions marking "500 years of resistance." Around this time, Zapatista speeches and literature on Indigenous power and identity worked their way around the globe, finding an eager audience in the North American and European libertarian movements. As David Graeber recalled about the Zapatistas, "who was listening to what they really had to say? Largely, it seems, a collection of teenage anarchists in Europe and North America, who soon began besieging the summits of the very global elite" who advocated neoliberalism and global capitalism.[38] Moreover, this drew many non-Indigenous activists in search of enlightenment to the Zapatista communities (*caracoles*). The North American fascination—sometimes bordering on exoticism—for these new Indigenous struggles was only heightened by episodes of armed resistance closer to home, including the Oka Crisis in Canada in 1990, the Ts'Peten/Gustafsen Lake standoff in 1995,[39] and the Caledonia land dispute[40] in 2006. It is therefore unsurprising that the

38   David Graeber, *Fragments of an Anarchist Anthropology* (Chicago: Prickly Paradigm Press, 2004), p. 105.

39   In 1995, after years of consensus regarding the shared use of lands that were an integral part of the ancestral territories of the Secwepemec people, tensions sprang up between an American rancher and a group of Indigenous people holding a Sun Dance ceremony. In August of that year, the Royal Canadian Mounted Police (RCMP) was called to secure the area. Following the refusal of the Indigenous group to leave the territory, the RCMP ran the most expensive paramilitary operation in Canadian history, complete with a media smear campaign against the Indigenous occupiers, whom they called terrorists, and a ban on journalists at the site. To this day, the federal government has ignored demands for a national inquiry into suspicions of corruption, excessive use of force and discrimination by the RCMP.

40   In 1995, the Six Nations took the Governments of Canada and Ontario to court for failing to respect a 1784 treaty reserving an area called the Haldimand Tract for the exclusive use of the community. A construction permit granted by the government to Henco Industries Ltd. triggered resistance from the women of the Six Nations community, who occupied the site, resulting in episodes of

anarchist groups that championed the alter-globalization movement of the late 1990s, triggered in part by the 1994 Zapatista uprising, would employ direct references to Indigenous struggles and decolonization, and that anarcho-indigenist and postcolonialist ideas would find their way into anarchist activist rhetoric.

Today

While many anarchists have expressed a fascination for Indigenous peoples and have sought confirmation of their own ideas in Indigenous beliefs and practices, Indigenous activists are seldom interested in anarchist knowledge, practices, and ideas, due in part to anarchism being branded as a white or settler ideology. Instead, they tend to find motivation to seek social justice in their own cultural experience. The aforementioned examples of armed Indigenous resistance in the 1990s and 2000s have inspired a generation of young Indigenous activists to take up the flag of political radicalism handed down to them by their elders. And this political radicalism, embedded in network such as the Mohawk Warrior Society or Rotisken'rakéhte, is neither hostile nor foreign to concepts of decentralized grassroots democracy, direct action, collective autonomy, ecological and anti-capitalist ideals, or, indeed, the refusal of entering into dialogue with the state.

As said before, proponents of the principles of liberty, equality, and solidarity, and especially anarchists, express not only a sensitivity to the precolonial history of Indigenous communities but also a real fascination with Indigenous culture, which has led some critics on the left to denounce anarchists for maintaining the utopist myth of the "noble

---

violence toward members of the Six Nations community by non-Indigenous residents of the area.

savage," or for attempting to reproduce a model of a set of societies that have disappeared for good. In a book devoted to refuting "libertarian thought," French anti-capitalist intellectual Frédéric Lordon castigates "libertarians" for their interest in the history of "Stateless societies" (a general term used to describe Indigenous societies). Lordon states that "the common error in all these plans to import *savagization* lies in our ignorance of the underlying variables, which are crucial to the viability of the model." This, he adds, can only lead to "a *delusional plan* to recreate this past in its entirety, with all its vestiges, which can be of *no use* to our contemporary lives" (our emphasis).[41] Some of these leftist critics tend to succumb to the same pitfalls they are railing against though; anti-capitalist philosophers and defenders of direct democracy such as Cornelius Castoriadis have also spread stereotypes about Indigenous communities, including the idea that they were trapped in permanent stagnation, prisoners of their own myths and norms. These judgments clearly say more about the prejudices and ignorance of those who express them than about the historical reality of Indigenous communities. Such critiques also ignore the fact that Indigenous peoples have indeed survived, that they exist in the present, and that they are still fighting colonialism while simultaneously taking on

41   Free translation from: Frédéric Lordon, *Imperium. Structures et affects des corps politiques* (Paris: La Fabrique, 2015), pp. 124–126. The author is critical of anthropological studies on the liberty, equality and solidarity of Indigenous communities or societies. Instead, he promotes accounts of "anthropological realism" (p. 255)—which he admits are fictional—inspired by the seventeenth-century English monarchist philosopher Thomas Hobbes, for whom the "natural state" referred to a situation where each person came into the world completely isolated (without parents, family, tribe, or clan) and where each person is against everyone else. Lordon states that in any community or society, a "governing State" must exist, and that "it is completely legitimate to talk about a tribe State, a city State, an empire State, a feudal State, an absolutist State, the modern State and the modern bourgeois State" (p. 123).

the state, the capitalist system, racism, and the patriarchy, sometimes with like-minded non-Indigenous anarchists protesting at their side, and sometimes not.

Is it possible to conceive of anarcho-indigenism in a way that does not involve pretending Indigenous communities are or ever were perfect, but rather that their history *and their present* offer elements that stimulate anarchist thought? To use the words of J. Kēhaulani Kauanui (see her interview later in the book), the idea isn't to force Indigenous peoples "to present proof that their way of life can be inspiring to anarchists," but rather "to evaluate how the criticism formulated by Indigenous peoples can help strengthen anarchist thought."

That said, it would be false to pretend that all current Indigenous activism is compatible with anarchism, and vice versa. As said before, "indigeneity" is always plural and does not fit within a homogeneous culture; the scholar field of "Indigenous studies" is rife with debates pertaining to the place of traditions within Indigenous identities, as well as the meaning of indigeneity; and any individual familiar enough with the inner life of Indigenous communities is fully aware of the depth of discussions taking place around how traditions should be carried on, how communities should be run and how relations with colonial authorities should be handled (see the interviews with Clifton Ariwakehte Nicholas and Freda Huson and Toghestiy).

Unfortunately, our knowledge of anarchist circles and of certain debates that shape and divide them—especially in Western Europe and the Americas—lead us to question the ability and the will of their adherents to hear the voices of the Indigenous activists in this book. While Indigenous communities and anarchists share a range of affinities, some experiences and concerns mentioned by the interviewees in these pages may be shocking to anarchist readers. In a text entitled "Locating an Indigenous Anarchism," Indigenous anarchist Aragorn! explains how certain anarchist tenets are indeed harmful to the development of a dialogue and respect between anarchists and Indigenous peoples.[42] He notes anarchists are often dogmatic and refuse to interact, at least politically, with people or groups that do not share their world vision and its vocabulary. He also points out many anarchists declare themselves to be against any form of identity politics, especially nationalism, while the struggle for decolonization is based on specific histories and cultural frameworks often associated with assertions of national identity. Furthermore, anarchists often claim to be atheists and reject any form of religion or spirituality, while spiritual practices and beliefs do have a central place in many Indigenous cultures, especially among women, as recalled by Erica Michelle Lagalisse in her depiction of Magdalena's marginalization while touring North American anarchist networks[43] (see also the interview with Véronique Hébert). Finally, anarchism tends to fall back onto the same linear progressive logic as Marxism and even liberalism, with the idea of time and history as a one-way street leading toward a better world, while Indigenous peoples tend to attach much greater importance to place, land, and territory. Although anarchism feeds from a wide variety of traditions, we must remind ourselves that the way we envision this type of praxis can hardly be dissociated from European histories and cultures, and therefore, in a way, from colonialism. It may be that, as a bridge between anarchist and Indigenous

---

42   Aragorn! "Locating an Indigenous Anarchism," in the collective work, *Uncivilized: The Best of Green Anarchy* (Green Anarchy Press, 2012), pp. 52–53.
43   Erica Michelle Lagalisse, "'Marginalizing Magdalena': Intersections of Gender and the Secular in Anarcho-indigenist Solidarity Activism," *Signs*, vol. 36, no. 3 (2011), pp. 653–678; and Sarita Ahooja, "Les anarchistes et la lutte pour l'autodétermination des Autochtones," in Rémi Bellemare-Caron *et al.* (eds.), *Nous sommes ingouvernables. Les anarchistes au Québec aujourd'hui* (Montreal: Lux, 2013), p. 199.

praxis, anarcho-indigenism may only be walkable by Indigenous people themselves, or in the words of Aragorn! that "the
only Indigenous anarchists that I have met (with one or three
possible exceptions) have been native people."[44]

In a similar vein, Adam J. Barker and Jenny Pickerill highlight that "anarchist practices do not *necessarily* lead to the
creation of decolonized social relations."[45] In our experience, seeing non-Indigenous anarchists trying to explain to
Indigenous people the best way to bring about the revolution without trying to understand their historical, political,
economic, social, and cultural realities is not uncommon.
Anarchist and anti-racist activist Sarita Ahooja (who participated in the Indigenous struggles in Bolivia, Chile, Guatemala,
and Mexico in the 1990s, as well as in the Six Nations struggle
against real estate development in Caledonia near Toronto in
2006) reminds us that

> the most important thing is to establish real contact with
> people, to invite them to take action together and to talk
> about things, rather than just showing up with your theories
> and concepts and saying that there is only one right way of
> doing things or of organizing. There are multiple ways of
> being an anarchist today.[46]

She encourages activists to step away from dogmatic ideologies and to be open to meeting people, sharing with them,
and talking about ideas and strategies, because that's the most
inspiring and stimulating thing about activism. It's not just

---

44   Aragorn! "Locating an Indigenous Anarchism," p. 55.
45   Adam J. Barker and Jenny Pickerill, "Radicalizing Relationships to and
through Shared Geographies: Why Anarchists Need to Understand Indigenous
Connections to Land and Place," *Antipode*, vol. 44, no. 5 (2012), p. 1716.
46   Free translation from: Ahooja, "Les anarchistes et la lutte pour l'autodétermination des Autochtones," p. 200.

about listening, according to Ahooja, but also about trying to hear, understand, and learn before passing judgment.

Yet, listening and understanding sometimes come with disenchantment; two years after this collection of interviews was first released in French in 2019, Klee Benally (a Diné – Navajo – musician of the rock band Blackfire, dancer of the group The Jones Benally Family and referring to himself as an "Indigenous anarchist"[47]) published "Unknowable: Against an Indigenous Anarchist Theory," in *Black Seed: Not on Any Map—Indigenous Anarchy in an Anti-Political World* (2021). In it, the author, who was also one of the organizers of the 2019 Indigenous Anarchist Convergence held in Kinłani (Flagstaff, Arizona), expressed firm doubts about the Eurocentric nature of anarchism, of course, but even about anarcho-indigenism in general, especially when stemming from academic networks:

> When anarchism speaks we locate an affinity in our hostility towards those who have imposed themselves upon us. But we resist to be reduced to political artifacts, so this has also made us hostile towards anarchist identity, though not entirely to anarchism [but] there is no Indigenous anarchist theory and perhaps there never should be [...]. [S]ettler colonizer anarchists in the so-called U.S. will always have to face this deep contradiction. Anarchism, or any other political proposition for that matter, simply cannot be imposed or "re-wilded" on stolen lands.

Then, the author went even further:

> Whether its performative allyship through land acknowledgments or adopting the label "accomplice," settlers need to implicate themselves fully into the destruction of their

---

47   To know more, see his website: http://kleebenally.com/about/.

social order. Otherwise [...] it's meaningless unless it is a position that informs every part of their analysis and actions, not just when a radical Indigenous moment occurs and they can attach their own analysis to it. [...] We reject the identifier of "anarcho-Indigenous" for this reason. We are not an appendage of a revolutionary ideology or strategy for power for someone else's existence. We do not seek to merely be acknowledged as a hyphen to anarchism or any liberation or resistance politics only to be subsumed into its counter movement against a dominant culture.

Hearing and listening to Indigenous people is and should be confrontational for non-Indigenous people. We (settlers) tend—and have the privilege to be able to do so—to forget or deny the extent with which our present lives would be impossible were it not for colonialism and its continuities. Far from being something of the past, colonialism is alive and well, and Europe and its Euro-American heirs are still reaping the benefits of stealing territories and destroying their occupants. Instead of fetishizing the struggle between cowboys and Indians or the ecological "grandeur" of Indigenous societies, we should be thinking carefully about the ways in which European nations continue to profit from this colonial history, and about the benefits some large port cities and capitals— Lisbon, London, Madrid, Paris—still enjoy as a result. This being said, the following interviews engage with these sensitive and somewhat difficult issues; as editors, we only hope they will foster reflection, dialogue, and, at best, solidarity and new struggles, while following the paths opened before us by zines such as *Accomplices Not Allies* (Indigenous Action Media, 2014), *Everyone Calls Themselves an Ally Until It Is Time to Do Some Real Ally Shit* (Ancestral Pride, 2014) and *When Being an Ally Turns Into Being an Appropriator* (Ancestral Pride, 2015). These three resources had the common purpose of offering an Indigenous point of view on the issue of relationships between Indigenous and non-Indigenous activists in the context of anti-colonial struggles and providing advice and criteria to non-Indigenous activists. They put forward ideas about what not to do when engaging in supportive advocacy, a list that includes such practices as: making declarations of solidarity without accepting the associated risk, rendering Indigenous activists invisible or appropriating their voices, tokenizing Indigenous activists, imposing particular strategies and tactics on a mobilization, or assuming an attitude of guilt and self-blame in order to ease a troubled conscience.

It is in this mindset of reconfiguring the anti-colonial struggle and of debating notions of cultural appropriation, privilege, colonialism, allyship, reciprocity, and support that we, as settlers living in Montreal-Tio'tia:ke/Mooniyang, have put together this collection of interviews. It is intended to be a modest contribution to actively encourage listening and dialogue in a trust-building process that will surely be complex, difficult, and potentially peppered with the misunderstandings that are bound to come up when two worlds collide.

We have conducted these interviews as settlers with anarchist leanings who wish to gather and distribute the words of half a dozen Indigenous individuals (as well as the specialist of indigenous people's history and politics Roxanne Dunbar-Ortiz, who is also a Marxist scholar) in an attempt to shed light on the notion of anarcho-indigenism, to make their views more accessible to and better heard by anarchists—and possibly by Indigenous communities as well—and to create a space for sharing ideas. This project does not offer any definitive answers nor a grand theory; instead, it puts forward a range of voices that express a wide variety of experiences and perspectives. These voices include activists, academics, and artists—and some individuals who are all of these at once. Many of the interviewees describe meetings with other Indigenous people, and most discuss the implications of the precolonial and colonial histories of their people and place emphasis on the importance of women within Indigenous political struggles. We hope that this book will kindle reflection and lead to further exchange, more discussion, and supportive collaboration. Finally, we would like to state that non-Indigenous people conducted most of the work involved in producing this book, including the preparation of interview transcripts, translation, editing, layout, and publishing.

Note about terminology

We use the term "Indian" only in reference to official texts (e.g. the Indian Act) or to highlight the derogatory nature of a comment or image. Please note that in Mexico, *Indigenism* is a government policy associated with the National Indigenist Institute, founded in 1948, which implemented and oversaw the control and assimilation Indigenous populations in Mexico. On the contrary, *Indianism* is an idea developed in Indigenous communities that has been espoused by progressive Central American anthropologists; it refers to concepts of Indigenous emancipation.[48]

---

48   Émilie-Emmanuelle Joly, *Droit à l'autodétermination des peuples indigènes et autogestion: le cas de la police communautaire dans l'État de Guerrero (Mexique)*, master's thesis, Department of Political Science, Université du Québec à Montréal, 2013.

Gord Hill

Anarcho-punk — anti-colonialism and anti-capitalism — solidarity — political violence — anarchism as a culture — survival in the wilderness — indigeneity in the Americas

Gord Hill is an Indigenous writer, artist, and activist from the Kwakwaka'wakw nation. He is the author and illustrator of *The 500 Years of Indigenous Resistance Comic Book* and *The Anti-Capitalist Resistance Comic Book* (both published by Arsenal Pulp Press in Vancouver, Canada), as well as the author of *500 Years of Indigenous Resistance* (edited by AK Press in Oakland, California) and *The Antifa Comic Book*. His art and writings have also been published in numerous periodicals, including *Briarpatch, Canadian Dimension, Redwire, Red Rising Magazine, The Dominion, Recherches Amerindiennes au Quebec, Intotemak, Seattle Weekly,* and *Broken Pencil*.

How did you find yourself being an anarchist and an Indigenous activist?

My first politicization was based on my work in Vancouver with a solidarity group for El Salvador, which supported the Farabundo Marti guerrilla movement against a US-backed regime. After this I began studying anarchist ideas and involving myself mostly with the anarchist punk movement, this was in the late 1980s and in Vancouver where I lived at that time this movement was still somewhat active. I was not very interested in Indigenous struggles until the 1990 Oka Crisis, and after this I began involving myself more with Indigenous resistance. Over the years I have maintained both anti-colonial and anti-capitalist resistance as my main orientation.

If you had to explain anarchism to someone in the easiest way possible, how would you do it? And indigenism?

I would say that anarchism is the belief that people do not need rulers or authorities to govern over them, and that it promotes decentralized and autonomous self-organization of movements and communities. As for indigenism, I don't use the term myself, but I would suggest it promotes a grassroots traditional approach in terms of organizing and methods. By traditional I mean those based on Indigenous culture and commonly used prior to colonization.

From what I've heard, the term anarcho-indigenism became popular in Canada thanks to Taiaiake Alfred. Yet, you were an anarchist long before he came up with it; has the idea of bringing together far-left ideals and indigenist thought become more popular over the last two decades according to you?

In a sense I would say yes, and this is what I term anti-colonial and anti-capitalist resistance, which are concepts that have been around since at least the late 1990s, I would say, at least in Canada. I don't really use the term anarcho-indigenism, nor do I see it used often. Overall, I believe that most Indigenous cultures are by nature decentralized and autonomous in terms of organization, without any centralized authorities or rulers. As for Taiaiake, I would not consider him an anarchist and I find his use of the term a little odd.

Following up on Alfred, one of his main points is he believes a revolution must start at first on the inside; his main goal, as he sees it himself, is to help people decolonize and re-indigenize themselves, as individual beings. On the other hand, I always had the feeling anarchists are keener to talk about big things (insurrection, fight against the state, smash capitalism) than personal behaviors, following the idea that insisting too much on the individual is part of the liberal philosophy and that it hides the general infrastructure of statism and capitalism. What's your take on this?

Taiaiake is partly influenced by Gandhi and liberal reformism, both of which tend to emphasize individual action such as boycotts, consumer choice, personal spiritual upliftment, etc. On the other hand, it's a basic understanding, I think, that revolutionaries need to transform themselves as a part of the revolutionary process, and certainly this would be the same as Indigenous people seeking liberation that, as people, they must work on decolonizing many aspects of their lives, including forms of organizing, lifestyle, diet, etc., because all this makes for a healthier and stronger people while contributing to the overall goal of liberation. But yes, there is, especially in "progressive movements" an over-emphasis on individual lifestyle choices and self-empowerment, with little acknowledgment of how difficult these processes can be within a capitalist system, or that the ultimate liberation will occur following the dismantling of the capitalist state.

It is acknowledged that some Indigenous people, such as official band councils' leaders, and private company owners, play by the rules of the colonial state and capitalism. They might even be proud of their political and financial "success." Yet, do you find that even Indigenous traditionalist activists and anarchists have internalized capitalist ideals and values? If so, what should be done about this?

I would say yes, because everyone who lives in a capitalist society is going to internalize capitalist ideology. Decolonization with an anti-capitalist consciousness seems to be the best way of countering capitalist ideology, as traditional culture and social organization generally promote collective or communal ways of life, sustainability, horizontal and autonomous organizing, etc. One of the problems I've seen in the past is Native activist types promoting decolonization but as capitalists, i.e. if we had our own corporations and financial self-sufficiency, etc., which just turns into more capitalist BS.

You were involved in the movement against the Winter Olympics in Vancouver back in 2010 (No Olympics on Stolen Native Land). It is also my understanding that, from an external viewpoint, there was a great solidarity between anarchists and warriors during the events. How did that work on the ground?

Beginning in early 2007 there emerged a more radical and militant campaign against the Olympics, involving Natives as well as anti-poverty activists in the city. Anarchists also began carrying out clandestine attacks on corporate and government targets, such as banks, military vehicles, etc. Over the course of the next three years this was basically how the campaign unfolded, with Natives and activists organizing most of the public direct actions and anarchists conducting a campaign of sabotage and vandalism. I think the clearest example of coordinating actions was on the day of the opening ceremonies on February 12, 2010, when around 5000 people rallied and marched against the Olympics. When we reached BC Place, the site of the ceremonies, the Native elders were at the front of the march but were then confronted with lines of riot police. Elders then asked the masked anarchists to go to the front, and there began an hours-long confrontation between anarchists and police, with pushing and shoving, etc. The next day there was the Heart Attack rally on the opening day of the games, during which an anarchist Black Bloc succeeded in carrying out some property destruction in the downtown business district, including smashing windows out of the Hudsons Bay Company department store. The Bay was a main partner in the Olympic Games of 2010 and also an important historical factor in the colonization of Canada.

You've been very vocal about the similarities between anarchism and the traditional warrior way (the masks, the insurrectionist ideal ...). Also, one of the most common representations of contemporary anarchism, the Black Bloc, plays a significant role in your comic book The Anti-Capitalist Resistance. *However, many liberal and even anarchist activists in North America and elsewhere claim that the Black Bloc tactic is mainly for white middle-class angry young men, and that people of color feel alienated by such a tactic. What is your take on this view?*

As a tactic the Black Bloc has emerged from predominantly white anarchist movements, such as those in Germany, but this doesn't mean it's only for angry white people anymore than an AK-47 designed by a white Russian guy is only for white people to use and carry. The Black Bloc also comes from a revolutionary perspective in that the capitalist system and its state institutions must be smashed. If people of color are alienated by such tactics I would assert it's largely because many movements are not revolutionary and are in fact reformist and even liberal. Having said that, you can see that in some "Third World" countries, such as Chile, Colombia, Brazil, and Egypt, the tactic of the Black Bloc has been adapted by revolutionaries, and they are neither white nor middle class as a whole.

From my experience as an activist within the anarchist movement in Quebec, I've witnessed some conflicts between anarchist and indigenist worldviews (on the use of national narratives, for instance). Have you experienced it, too, in BC?

I've compared the anarchist ideal of decentralized and autonomous self-organization with the traditional forms of social organization most Indigenous peoples used, in which there were no formal rulers or centralized authority. As for militant anarchists, I've compared them to the Indigenous warrior in that they use militant action to defend people or carry out attacks. Certainly there are conflicts in BC as well between these movements, primarily I think due to cultural and tactical differences. In many confrontations, for example, Native peoples are generally very cautious in how these conflicts are carried out, because actions taken can have a big impact on their community, their families, etc. Many anarchists, on the other hand, tend to promote militant actions as a first choice in part because they will be less affected by the consequences, with some exceptions of course. Then again, you will also find rather conservative views among many Native people, including those who participate in protests, who are opposed to any militant actions by either warriors or anarchists, as well as Natives who will work with police while organizing a rally. Many of the same dynamics non-Native radicals have to contend with are also at play in Native communities.

You always associate yourself with the anti-colonial and anti-capitalist movement. What do you think of other trends, such as radical or anarcha-feminism, and also anarcho-ecologism and anti-specism, which is very dynamic on the West Coast among the anarchist milieu?

I don't have very much association or interaction with people who promote these specific types of ideals, and some may be more centered on the US West Coast as opposed to here in western Canada. I think all these radical/revolutionary milieus have something to offer in terms of critiques of the capitalist and colonial system as I understand it, and within the anarchist movement their contributions have certainly helped expand people's consciousness and understanding of the society we live in, even if we don't all subscribe to their specific labels.

You said once that you see anarchists almost as a specific tribe, with its own culture. What would be the reluctance toward anarchism we might find among Indigenous people, and even Indigenous activists?

I think there are some significant cultural differences between anarchists and Indigenous peoples. Anarchists tend to be more individualistic, and they also adopt a lot of what appear to be "bizarre" lifestyles to Native peoples, such as eating out of dumpsters, rejecting personal hygiene, etc. Not all anarchists engage in these activities, but I think a good number do and they are the most visible cultural traits an outsider might observe about "typical" anarchist groups. Many Native activists I think see anarchists as a variation of "hippies" and punks. It reminds me of what a Native elder once told a group of us, that when you begin the process of decolonizing you will become different from your people. That's a good thing, but if we go too far in our personal decolonization we may risk alienating and appearing foreign to our communities, which can limit our ability to engage with them and participate in common struggles. I think many anarchists are on this road, and appear and act radically different from what would be their own communities, so anarchism becomes a highly insular movement that in some ways focuses inwardly on its own lifestyles and activities ... Another aspect of this is the anti-social character of the North American anarchist movement, where many participants hate and reject the society and become further estranged from it the more they are involved in the movement, perpetuating the marginalization of the movement. Native activists are generally focused on working with their communities, building solidarity with other movements, etc., but are not coming at it from such an anti-social perspective.

What about veganism?

Yes, veganism would certainly be one of those cultural differences, although there are not a lot of vegans that I know of in the anarchist movement (here in BC). And, of course, veganism is somewhat of an "alien" concept to Indigenous peoples who traditionally hunted and fished, practices that are still widespread and common.

Your comments are really interesting, however, you said that you came yourself to activism through the punk movement … Thus, how do you find a balance between your own countercultural posture and your relatives and your Native community?

I think at first it was odd for my family but over the years more of my cousins, etc., were involved in countercultural types of activities, and when I really looked at the punk scene there were actually quite a few Natives involved, they just never identified as Natives … the same is true in the anarchist movement to some extent in that there are quite a few Natives participating but their Indigenous identity is not central to their politics …

Do you consider yourself a bridge builder between the anarchist and the Native community? And if so, is it a one-way or a two-way bridge?

Not really, I do promote anarchist actions and tactics as well as the concepts of autonomous self-organization, because at the end of the day I'm not trying to recruit Natives into an anarchist movement but rather promote the best practices of anarchists so that Natives can learn from other's experiences.

How do you deal with the fact that Euro-American anarchists are settlers themselves, and white more often than not?

This is of course the result of European colonization of the Americas. How I deal with it is by trying to understand this history and the dynamics it creates when participating in resistance movements, while acknowledging there is a need for multinational resistance and solidarity between social movements, especially in North America.

From what you tell on your blog and all the information you share about knives, survival, etc., you seem to know your territory quite well, and how to live on it. Now, it seems to me that when it comes to living in the wild ("off the grid"), most of those who get into that sort of thing within the settler world are called preppers/survivalists, with all the bad press and the accusations of right-winged extremism it's been associated with (accusations that I don't necessarily condone). Personally, I've always had the impression that, more often than not, anarchists were city-dwellers, contrary to most warriors. Any thoughts on that, and how it might bear on the solidarity between anarchists and warriors?

Yes, I would agree, most warrior types are not living in the cities, while most anarchists are. At the same time there are considerable numbers of anarchists who also live in rural areas and who are acquiring various wilderness/survival skills, at least here in BC. In regards with relations between anarchists and warriors in general there are always differences between people living in cities and those living in rural areas, both for Natives and non-Natives. Additionally, if we look at the history of Indigenous resistance movements since the 1960s, most of these have at first originated in urban areas, as in many regions around half the Native population live in urban areas.

You were in the military, in the reserve, when you were younger, like Taiaiake Alfred, who was a Marine, in the US military. Why did you get in, and why did you quit, and what do you think now about this experience?

Yes, I was in an infantry reserve regiment based in Vancouver. And before this I was in the Army Cadets for five years as a teenager, so that was how I ended up in the reserves. I had planned on joining the regular forces and being an airborne soldier, as I had already completed a basic parachutist course at CFB Edmonton. I quit the military after being exposed to anarchist punk and going to shows, and just generally expanding my mind and learning about the world we live in, and the oppressive role of military forces in maintaining it. Personally, I think it was a good experience in that I learned many useful skills, including field craft, small arms, tactics, organizing, self-discipline, etc.

In your comic book, The 500 Years of Resistance, *you tell the story of the Indigenous pan-American resistance movement to colonization. What would be your relation toward Indigenous movements in the south, in the so-called Latin American countries, or even in other places, such as Aotearoa?*

I think Indigenous peoples around the world generally share a similar philosophy or worldview. In the Americas there is a significant language barrier between north and south, so that can limit the building of a strong relationship. I think Native peoples in North America, because of the similar experience with English colonialism, also tend to form stronger relations with Indigenous people from regions also colonized by the British, such as Australia and Aotearoa. You can see in regard to Indigenous tribal peoples in Asia or Africa where we have far less contact or knowledge of their situation. On the Pacific coast we've also had stronger relations with Aotearoa people in general due to the similarities in culture (i.e. ocean-going canoes, carving, etc.).

In a conference on anarchism and Indigenist resistance, that you delivered in Montreal, at La Déferle, on May 19, 2013, you explained that there were several types of political and social Indigenous organizations in America before the European colonization, but that those which would be said to have been more anarchist, i.e. decentralized and egalitarian, resisted longer than the others to colonization. Could you develop this idea a bit more?

Yes, I think that was a reference to different forms of social organization, one being more centralized and the other not. The specific examples were of the Mexica (Aztec) who had a large civilization with millions of citizens and many warriors, but who were quickly defeated by a few hundred Spanish conquistadors allied with thousands of people who had been subjugated by the Mexica. Their rulers were captured and the empire collapsed, along with a massive disease epidemic that decimated the Mexica. Another similar example would be the Inca. On the other hand, you had decentralized and autonomous societies, such as those on the Great Plains (including the Lakota, Cheyenne, etc.) who waged guerrilla warfare over several decades against the US military, or in South America the Mapuche, who were also decentralized and autonomous and who were never defeated by the Spanish for a period of some three hundred years. So the lesson here is that a centralized, authoritarian structure is easily defeated through decapitation, while autonomous resistance movements are much more difficult to destroy because there is no center to be attacked.

What prospect do you see? For the anarchists? For native warriors? For the solidarity between both?

I generally promote a multinational resistance movement that is both anti-colonial and anti-capitalist. Overall, there is a need for solidarity between many social sectors. I think as socio-economic conditions continue to decline, as people become more conscious and determined, there is a great potential for resistance movements to expand.

Roxanne Dunbar-Ortiz

Interviewed by Ragina Johnson and Brian Ward[1]

American Indian Movement (AIM) — Wounded Knee incident — Black Power and struggle against apartheid — history of New Mexico — Marxism and colonialism — First Peoples and the working class — the anarchists — franchise and settler colonialism

Roxanne Dunbar-Ortiz is Professor Emerita of Ethnic Studies at California State University, and she is the author of *An Indigenous Peoples' History of the United States* (2014). She grew up in Oklahoma and during the 1960s took part in the anti-war movement and became a member of the militant feminist organization Cell 16, which became well known for encouraging celibacy, separation from men, and self-defense training. She later joined the American Indian Movement and the International Indian Treaty Council in 1974. Her first book, *The Great Sioux Nation: An Oral History of the Sioux Nation and its Struggle for Sovereignty*, was published in 1977 as the founding document of the first international conference on Indians of the Americas, which was held the same year at the United Nations headquarters in Geneva. During the 1980s, Dunbar-Ortiz made more than a hundred trips to Nicaragua and Honduras to appraise the territorial conflicts surrounding the ancestral rights of the Miskitos

1   First published in *ISR International Socialist Review*, no. 103. Thanks to the editors and to Roxanne Dunbar-Ortiz for the authorization to republish this interview.

Indians and to monitor the war taking place between the Sandinistas and the US-backed Contras. Since then, she has written extensively on the topics of Indigenous struggles for self-determination and territorial politics, notably in her autobiographical trilogy *Red Dirt: Growing Up Okie, Outlaw Woman: A Memoir of the War Years, 1960–1975,* and *Blood on the Border: A Memoir of the Contra War.*

Among other influences, Dunbar-Ortiz was brought to Marxist history by Howard Adams, a Métis activist and historian who authored *Prison of Grass: Canada from a Native Point of View* (2nd edition, 1989). She also authored the introduction to the collective book *Quiet Rumours: An Anarcha-Feminist Reader,* where she self-identifies as an anarcha-feminist: "Our task as anarcha-feminists can be nothing less than changing the world and to do that we need to consult our heroic predecessors, such as Louise Michel, Lucy Parsons, Mother Jones, Emma Goldman, Helen Keller and Azucena Fernandez Barba." Following this, her work addresses the interconnections between capitalism and colonialism, as well as the potential light Marxism and anarchism can shed on the past and present Indigenous struggles in the Americas.

Could you tell us some of your history as an activist and how you got involved in these issues?

I came into the American Indian Movement (AIM) a few years after it was founded, in 1973 during Wounded Knee II. I had been involved at San Francisco State in the early 1960s and things were beginning to rumble there during the civil rights movement. I was married and a working-class student. The left seemed like an elite crew to me, and I couldn't find anyone to relate to until some African American students invited me to come to a Du Bois Club meeting that had started there at SF State.

Then I went to UCLA and there was a big Du Bois Club in Los Angeles. Of course, it was a Communist Party affiliate. I was mainly involved in Latin American history as a graduate student, specifically the anti-imperialist and anti-apartheid movements, because African studies and Latin American studies crossed over a lot [in] supporting national liberation movements. That was the main context for my politics, and Marxism was not that popular in the New Left. I personally loved the old communists and thought they were great. I loved listening to their stories, especially the labor struggles. My grandfather had been in the Industrial Workers of the World (IWW) in Oklahoma. This was the ideological setting that I had in my mind, but I couldn't quite understand the New Left, and why they wanted to avoid Marxist theory, because I didn't understand anti-communism and the Cold War yet.

During this time, I was doing my academic research. I ended up finally writing my dissertation in 1974. I was in residence at UCLA for three years. Then I went off to be a full-time revolutionary until I decided to teach. But I was with the Latin American students, who were mostly Mexican American, and not at all allergic to Marxism, coming from the Mexican revolutionary tradition. I was exposed to a lot, and I became more of an activist during the anti-Vietnam War movement. I learned some organizing skills, and toward the end of my time at UCLA we were trying to organize a teaching assistants' union. The union was formed after I left, and I felt I had helped lay the foundations for that.

In the summer of 1967, I went off to London to work with the African National Congress (ANC). I was there for three months and this was the first time I ever met real revolutionaries [at the] ANC world headquarters. Getting to know the ANC and learning from its experiences was quite sobering after three years at university, and what felt like mainly talk. Instead, everything had consequences for the ANC.

That was an important learning experience, and the ANC wanted me to stay and work with them. They had recruited a number of people who did stay and I sometimes regret that I did not stay. After leaving London, I visited some of the veterans of the Vietnam War who had deserted the war effort and were living in Geneva, Switzerland. I decided I had to go back to the United States and get involved in the revolution, because everyone would be needed. I felt that there wasn't all that much I could contribute to the ANC because I had no direct connections.

I was also becoming more and more troubled by male chauvinism in the movement. It was clear it was in the general society, but I romanticized the movement, especially the ANC, and thought they were better than that. Returning to the United States and organizing in the Boston area, I got angrier and angrier at men in the Students for a Democratic Society (SDS) and the anti-draft movement, the motto of which was, "Girls say yes to boys who say no." I hadn't felt oppressed so much directly, but of course I was, although I had been treated as a kind of "honorary" man. Once I started taking a feminist stand I got condemned. It was pretty hard to take at the time. And male chauvinism had terrible consequences for the women's movement and for the development of the left, because it took some of the strongest feminists out of the left and made the left unwelcoming to newly politicized young women.

How did you get involved in AIM and make connections with the broader left at the time?

I finished my dissertation at UCLA on the history of land tenure in New Mexico's Indigenous practices from the precolonial era to the mid-twentieth century, then took a teaching position in a new Native American Studies program at Cal

State Hayward [today known as California State University, East Bay]. Even while writing my dissertation the year before, I got involved with the Wounded Knee Legal Defense/Offense committee, which was based in South Dakota but had a large contingent in the San Francisco Bay area. Two of the main lawyers on the hundreds of criminal cases that stemmed from arrests following the Wounded Knee siege, John Thorne and Vine Deloria Jr., asked me to serve as an expert witness at a hearing to dismiss the remaining Wounded Knee cases, based on the Sioux–US Treaty of 1868, which maintained Sioux sovereignty over all that transpired in their treaty territory. I was no expert on Native American treaties, but Vine Deloria Jr. guided me to the literature. At the two-week hearing held in federal court in Lincoln, Nebraska, I served as an expert witness but also as part of the legal team. Ninety percent of the testimony from Sioux elders provided the oral history of the Sioux nation, their treaty with the United States, and the wars that followed, culminating in the 1890 US Army massacre of unarmed Sioux refugees. At the end of the hearing, the elders asked me to turn the court transcripts into an oral history of the Great Sioux Nation, which I worked on for the following three years, publishing the book by that name in 1977.[2]

Soon, I got involved in the project AIM developed with the elders, with the founding of the International Indian Treaty Council, to go to the United Nations with the Sioux treaty. In 1977 we had the first international meeting, and the rest of my time in the Indigenous movement has mainly been that international work, which continues to this day. The movement developed over three decades, culminating in success in the UN General Assembly's 2007 Declaration on the Rights of Indigenous Peoples, and has tripled in participation since then.

---

2   *The Great Sioux Nation: Sitting in Judgment on America* (Lincoln: Bison Books, 2013).

Now back to AIM itself. AIM was in the "rainbow coalition" with other organizations like the Black Panther Party, the Puerto Rican Young Lords, the Chicano Crusade for Justice, and other organizations. AIM was founded in 1968, in Minneapolis, just one year before the occupation of Alcatraz. The founders were Ojibwa, but the movement spread throughout the country. This was all in the context of the civil rights movement and rise of the Black Panther Party. The uprising at Alcatraz was pretty much grassroots and organized by urban Indians in the Bay Area and Native students, especially at San Francisco State, where the Third World liberation movement and strike took place in 1968.[3] A Native student, Richard Oakes, was one of the leaders of the strike and a leader in the liberation of Alcatraz in 1969. John Trudell, who would become the chairman of AIM, was another leader at Alcatraz. But the leadership of Native women such as LaNada War Jacket, Madonna Thunder Hawk, and Lorelei DeCora was the essential element that allowed the community to remain for 18 months.

The struggles of Indigenous people have a rich history, and really came together in the struggles of the 1960s and 1970s with other movements for liberation. In your books, it's clear you are making the connection between land dispossession, labor, and class—basically Marx's approach of historical materialism. You even quoted Marx from Capital *in the beginning of the second chapter, entitled "Culture of Conquest." Why is this approach important to struggles for liberation?*

---

3   The Third World Liberation Front was a broad coalition of Chicano, Native American, Asian American, and African American students who organized against institutional racism on campuses, and successfully won the College of Ethnic Studies at San Francisco State College.

I think Marxism is a hard sell in the Native movement and for African Americans but less so for Mexican Americans because of their political genealogies. Today it's even difficult for Chicanos, as well as Native Americans, because Marxism is deemed just Western epistemology or a Western world-view. There is of course a lot of Eurocentrism in Marx's early writings. There is the idea of progress, but people don't look at his later work enough, when he was getting into ethnolo-gy.[4] He didn't know much about non-European peoples, yet making generalities about the whole world can seem imperi-alist. However, I found out when I was doing my dissertation, that using Marxism to look at the history of land tenure in New Mexico at different stages from Spanish colonization through US conquest and colonization was essential. Marx describes the initial looting of the Americas as reckless abandon, as well as the enslavement of Africans, and the genocide of Native Americans, and this describes the initial Spanish invasion and occupation of New Mexico, which led to the All Indian Pueblo Revolt driving the Spanish colonists out for more than a decade.[5] The second period of eighteenth-century Spanish colonialism was far more of a negotiated relationship. It was still colonialism, but it wasn't the most vicious kind, and the Spanish army was there to defend that zone from French and British expansion.[6]

---

4   Karl Marx in his later years wrote ethnological notebooks looking at pre-capitalist societies, including studying the Iroquois in North America. Marx didn't live long enough to complete this study. It was later published under co-authors Karl Marx and Lawrence Krader, *The Ethnological Notebooks of Karl Marx: Studies of Morgan, Phear, Maine, Lubbock* (Assen: Van Gorcum, 1972).

5   This is known as the Pueblo Revolt of 1680, led by Popé, which succeeded in pushing out the Spanish for twelve years before they reconquered the area.

6   This area of the southwest United States is often referred to as the bor-derlands. Gloria Anzaldúa defined this area as a zone that is not fully the US or Mexico and can go in between both cultural worlds. See Gloria Anzaldúa, *Borderlands/La Frontera* (San Francisco: Aunt Lute Books, 1999). Jeremy Adel-

Through the history of Mexico becoming independent and then New Mexico being taken by the US, I tried to look at capitalist development and to link this with imperialism. I read all kinds of things from Marx and participated in Marxist study groups. At the time I hadn't done a real study of *Capital*. I started reading about Oriental despotism, and Marx's analysis of how the pyramids were built. These grand public works were built by forced labor, and I connected that to what I was seeing in precolonial Indigenous New Mexico—they had elaborate irrigation systems, which were also throughout Mexico and Central America. You have almost a dictatorship to control water, but the way Indigenous peoples organized it was with serial dictatorships. The ditch boss would be elected for one year and had total control of the water in each pueblo. These 98 city-states along the Rio Grande and its tributaries also went to war with each other periodically over water, so it could be very serious. They could starve as a result of being in the desert. With the water supply, they had an absolute autocratic ditch boss and everyone had to contribute labor. There wasn't a class of laborers, and after a year the ditch boss could never again be in that position. It had to change every year so that they didn't get used to the power.

This history shows how people can organize themselves in different ways; capitalism and exploitative labor were not inevitable in human history. Just because capitalism came to dominate the world through European and United States imperialism, forcing the world to live under capitalism does

man and Stephen Aron argue in their essay "From Borderlands to Borders" how borderlands were more fluid culturally and ethnically. Indigenous people cohabited with non-Natives and retained some of their power prior to the solidification of the US and Mexico nation-state borders. See Jeremy Adelman and Stephen Aron, "From Borderlands to Borders: Empires, Nation-States, and the Peoples in between in North American History," *The American Historical Review*, vol. 104, no. 3 (1999), 814–841.

not mean it was inevitable. We need to build upon Marx's brilliant comprehension of how capitalism arose in Europe and how it works. But the social and political systems that produced ancient irrigation systems and widespread agricultural production in the Americas were not despotic.[7] It has been said the beginning of the class system started in ancient Egypt, but I found things that didn't fit that mold. I tried to apply the basic tenets of Marxism and especially what is known as "primitive accumulation."

I want to mention here that there are a lot of words Marx used that should be retranslated. For instance, regarding primitive accumulation, it's just easy to say "primary" or "higher" but Marxists don't know what you're talking about unless you say primitive. In other languages, primitive means primary.[8] It doesn't necessarily have the baggage that the word "primitive" does for Indigenous peoples subjected to European ethnography. It became clear to me while working on my thesis that the first big onslaught of the primitive accumulation process that set off capitalist development happens over and over again, even today. This has entered into a part of Native studies with Glen Coulthard's book, *Red Skin, White Masks*, in which he makes that argument.[9] Coulthard identifies with the anarchist tendency, but he takes on Ward Churchill's piece in *Marxism and Native Americans*.[10] Coulthard says it's ridiculous to not use such an important tool as Marx's work.

---

7   There are many precapitalist economic formations that don't conform to Karl Marx's model of Oriental despotism, and in fact Marx changed how he described some precapitalist societies in his later writing. This is detailed in Kevin Anderson, *Marx at the Margins: On Nationalism, Ethnicity, and Non-Western Societies* (Chicago: University of Chicago Press, 2010).

8   During Karl Marx's writing of *Capital* his use of the word "primitive" meant primary or first rather than stating inferiority of cultures. Karl Marx, *Capital: A Critique of Political Economy* (New York: Penguin Books, 1990).

9   Published by University of Minnesota Press in 2014.

10   Ward Churchill published a book of essays in 1983 for South End Press

In all my work, I try to apply historical materialism. However, I don't think any of the original Marxists and following generations of European Marxists dealt with colonialism as the avatar of capitalism. Lenin theorized imperialism, but he dealt with it in the most technical way of financial capital, which is really important. And he did deal with national liberation. But I don't think Marx or Lenin even began to understand the role the US was playing throughout the nineteenth century as the vortex of capitalism, and what I try to show is that from the very beginning the United States was based on colonial conquest, and on overseas imperialism following their independence from the British Empire.

As we have been diving into current debates and writings from the left, we have found an absence of analysis on the question of Native Americans and labor. You mentioned Glen Coulthard earlier and he actually says in the introduction of Red Skin, White Masks,

> *It appears that the history of* dispossession, *not proletarianization, has been the dominant background structure shaping the character of the historical relationship between Indigenous peoples and the Canadian state … Stated bluntly, the theory and practice of Indigenous anti-colonialism, including Indigenous anti-capitalism, is best understood as a struggle primarily inspired by and oriented around the question of land … and less around our emergent status as "rightless proletarians."*

But in fact, you have talked about many Native Americans being part of the working class as you mention recently in your Real News interview.[11] Why is this?

---

called *Marxism and Native Americans*, which counterposes indigeneity to Marxism. The latter, however, is represented in the collection largely by Maoist authors. Churchill's lead essay argues that Marxism is a European ideology that is alien to Native American culture.

11 The Real News Network interview with Roxanne Dunbar-Ortiz in October of 2014, www.youtube.com/watch?v=3JDxZ6PMFeA.

For instance, in the Diné nation (Navajo reservation) the energy industry has long dominated, and in the 1970s, Navajos formed trade unions to demand that they have the jobs and job training. In the early part of the twentieth century, Navajos and Pueblo Indians made up much of the workforce on the railroads that ran through their territories in the southwest. In the federal government's relocation program of the 1950s and 1960s, half the reservation and rural population migrated to urban areas for jobs in industry; however, many had moved on their own during the war to work in the defense industry. I think ignoring this is a problem for some academics. Some of the Native people in academia come from more prosperous families. I don't believe any Native person is super wealthy; even in the biggest casinos the money is distributed and there is not a real ruling class—but there are definitely class issues in terms of consciousness. All the AIM activists were from working-class families, but are no less Lakota, Diné, or Salish because of it. They worked at all kinds of jobs. So for me, I felt really comfortable in AIM because it was working class and people were not ashamed to be workers. In fact they were quite proud, and they were drawn to unions when anyone bothered to organize them.

When the Navajo workers began to organize in the 1970s with the United Mine Workers, it was against federal law for unions to organize on Indian reservations. Peter McDonald[12] challenged that and won. The Navajo workers had specific demands for medical benefits; they bargained to include their medicine men to be paid. They had the Indian Health Service, but they wanted to pay their medicine people and were able to get this into their contract. They are very strong union people. Unfortunately, there are other problems with the fossil fuel

---

12   Peter McDonald was a Diné code talker in World War II and was the first elected Tribal Chairman of the Diné nation (Navajo reservation) in 1970.

industry and internal struggles in reservations over ending extraction for environmental reasons.

I think Coulthard is trying to say that exploitation and expropriation are different things. But all capitalism starts with *expropriation* of land from the producers, and not just in the Americas but as the prerequisite for the development of capitalism in Europe. That's what I describe as the culture of conquest in my book, about the commons being fenced in and that *all* expropriation started with the land.

We've been trying to use Marxism as the framework to talk about Indigenous issues. If you merely say Marxism is European, you miss the point of the theory. People forget that Marx actually talked about who was expropriated, how people were actually dispossessed, and how that created the material basis ultimately for colonization, and how the vast majority of settlers and migrants who came to the US ended up in factories as low-wage workers.

I worked hard on the first chapter of my book about the pre-colonial era in the Americas, where there were prosperous and urban civilizations without capitalism, and that is so hopeful. Most radical forms of anarchism now are anti-civilization, and they often look to Native people as the inspiration. They use Indigenous peoples, especially Native people in the Americas, pulling out what they want to justify their ideology. They are creating fantasies as evidence and even calling it science. Anarchists, especially the primitivists, view agriculture as the basis of all evil, because they are looking at agribusiness, and they don't want to know at all that 90 percent of Native people in the Western hemisphere were agriculturalists—they don't want to know that fact. So they romanticize Native people as "hunter-gatherers."

This viewpoint distorts the reality in the Western hemisphere. The civilizations of central Mexico and the Andes were still developing before the Europeans intervened. The civilizations of the Americas were going in a different direction than Europe or Asia. I think had Marx really been able to study or know what was hardly even knowable at that time, he would have said that capitalism in the Americas was not inevitable. I always say that 500 years ago with the invasion of the Americas, a wrong path was taken for humanity. So let's say that capitalism is wrong and destructive, not that it was inevitable. For example, with the ancestral Puebloans, it was clearly a choice. They had a large civilization up on Mesa Verde [in present day Colorado]; they had irrigation ditches for miles and were overusing the wood, because everything was built of wood. They were probably becoming less democratic, and they made the choice to migrate to the Rio Grande area of northern New Mexico and break down into smaller villages. They continued to function like city-states, but they were smaller than the one large civilization up at Mesa Verde. And why not say that was a choice and just maybe that the Americas were going in a different direction, rather than interpreting this or the Maya devolvement as "collapse?" This is something to learn from: civilization without capitalism and how can it work. This is tied with the concept of humans being a part of nature; for example, conventional Marxist thinking argues that private property began with the domestication of animals in Africa. However, in America the ancestral peoples did not domesticate animals for food or as beasts of burden. In the civilizations of Central America, parrots and dogs were domesticated but were considered sacred. The Spanish invaders noted that the Aztec dogs did not bark, but they learned to bark from the Spanish war dogs.

Can you talk more about the relationship between settler colonialism and capitalism? What do you define as settler colonialism?

Anarcho-Indigenism

What is the difference between settler colonialism and outpost colonialism?

Yes, it is really important. I am not sure I entirely succeed in the book on this because the tendency of European-based Marxism is to separate the two, and of course in the United States they are like two separate worlds. Because of Lenin, we have a good connection between capitalism and imperialism, and most people assume the connection. But with colonialism, bourgeois history tends to call things colonialism that weren't colonialism, such as the Roman Empire. Yes, they had colonies, but it wasn't capitalist based. It was a different era; so people like to say "people have been colonizing each other forever," but colonialism is just a different system under capitalism. In settler colonialism, Europeans export people with the promise of land, and private property, so that land itself becomes the chief commodity in the primitive accumulation of capital, and in North America, colonists also enslaved Africans as both market commodities and unpaid and unfree labor. This is a distinct form of colonialism, which obviously proved to be the most effective in building the most powerful capitalist state, the United States. The main form of European colonialism was to exploit resources—precious metals, African bodies, spices—in which Native labor was organized with European overseers and bureaucrats, as well as Native middlemen. This form of colonialism, of course, produced great wealth for the European monarchies and later European states, and created the structures of unequal global markets that persist today.

I want to make clear that there is not one "settler colonial" or "colonial" experience. Each has to be analyzed on its own terms, depending on many factors, such as which colonial state and which period of time is being considered. The European fetish for gold that developed during the Middle Ages drove nearly all of the early colonial ventures, but rare spices were also worth their weight in gold. And most importantly, the study of any colonial situation requires understanding the level and nature of resistance to these invasions. In making general conclusions regarding the Anglo and Anglo-American colonization of North America, it is essential to keep in mind that each of the hundreds of Native nations had a unique experience of colonialism, always destructive, but varying in details and survivability.

It's inaccurate to speak, for instance, of "the California Indians." The eighteenth-century Spanish colonization of the coastal region from San Diego to San Francisco was carried out by Franciscan missionaries with the use of the Spanish army in seizing people in the whole region to be incarcerated in the missions, and to work for the missionaries in their commercial pursuits. So these weren't typical settlers, but it was settler colonialism. On the other hand, the nearly half of California north of San Francisco was not colonized until the United States confiscated the northern part of what had become Mexico, and the rush of settlers arrived as gold-seekers with the 1850s gold rush. These were not typical settlers either, combining extraction with genocide.

Colonialism in general is disruptive, destructive, damaging, sometimes depopulating entire areas, such as the Natchez villagers of the Mississippi Delta and the Nahuatl-speaking villagers of western Nicaragua and western Honduras who were seized by Spanish slave traders in the sixteenth century, then transported to work in the mines of Peru. European settlers didn't arrive to those nearly depopulated areas until later. This was similar to the way villagers of West Africa were captured, enslaved, and sold in the Americas, losing their existence as particular nations and peoples.

I would say that settler colonialism was an exceptional mode of colonialism. English settler colonialism in the North American colonies took its specific form from the mid-seventeenth-century English conquest of Ireland, in which English forces under Oliver Cromwell drove subsistent Irish farmers off their land and gave land grants to English and Scottish settlers. The developing English capitalism based in the wool industry required surplus labor to work in the factories, as well as large swaths of grazing land for commercial sheep production. The process of fencing the commons and driving English farmers off the land created that surplus labor force, but also a pool of settlers who were promised free land in America. The Protestant Anglos and Scots, who settled Northern Ireland, made up the majority of frontier settlers in the British North American colonies.

The Portuguese and the Spanish were specifically seeking gold and silver. Their hoarding of gold and silver actually limited their ability to develop capitalism. They didn't really have a basis for that in the Iberian Peninsula after they deported all the farmers, craftsmen, architects, and other producers who were Muslims and Jews. Only in the eighteenth century did Spain begin establishing settler-colonies in the southern cone of South America, employing the same genocidal methods of eliminating or driving out the Indigenous peoples, which continued when Argentina, Chile, and Uruguay became independent.

However, only the United States developed effective capitalism outside of Britain. By 1840, it was already the largest economic power in the world on the basis of the global cotton trade and textile factories, also providing cotton to the British textile industry. Until recently, economic historians have dated the development of US capitalism to post–Civil War industrialization in the north. Several recent books have convincingly made the case for the cotton kingdom in the Mississippi Valley being the site of the birth of full-blown capitalism prior to the Civil War, based on slave labor and the capital generated by the value of the slaves' bodies.[13] This development included the parallel expulsion of the five large Native agricultural nations from the southeast during the 1830s and 1840s, generating huge amounts of capital in land sales.

Related to this, do you see a difference between Coulthard and your mentor Howard Adams on these questions and how they view Marxism and socialism in relation to Native people?

Having read both of them, I would say first that Coulthard identifies with anarchism. But unlike many anarchists, he is not at all allergic to using aspects of Marxist theory, and he criticizes the idea of dismissing Marxist ideas and arguments. Most important, he identifies capitalism as an enemy of Indigenous self-determination. In his extraordinary book *Red Skin, White Masks*, he writes, "For Indigenous nations to live, capitalism must die. And for capitalism to die, we must actively participate in the construction of Indigenous alternatives to it."

In that respect, Coulthard and Adams are the same. They both argue that capitalism must die for Indigenous peoples to be free. But at the same time, Coulthard does not recognize the proletarian nature of most Native people's lives for the past several centuries. I understand that his research is grounded in Dene reality.

Howard Adams,[14] on the other hand, grounded his research in the Métis world. In his classic work *Prison of Grass*, he

13   See: Sven Beckert, *Empire of Cotton: A Global History* (New York: Alfred A. Knopf, 2014); Edward Baptist, *The Half Has Never Been Told: Slavery and the Making of American Capitalism* (New York: Basic Books, 2014); and Walter Johnson, *River of Dark Dreams: Slavery and Empire in the Cotton Kingdom* (Cambridge, MA: Belknap Press, 2013).

14   Howard Adams was a Métis activist and author of *Prison of Grass: Canada from a Native Point of View* (Toronto: Fifth House Publishers; 2nd ed., 1989).

combines autobiography and the history of the Métis; he characterizes the greatest uprising of Indigenous peoples in Canada and maybe all of North America as a workers' struggle as well as being an anti-colonial struggle. This was the revolution, led by Louis Riel, against the exploitation of the Métis workers in the fur trade, as well as the encroachments into Native territories.[15] And, of course, in Mexico and in the Andean region, Indigenous labor is the primary exploited labor. In fact, Native individuals were primarily workers in the colonial economic systems that existed in the US and Canada. They are not significantly a part of the 1 percent: they are workers. A person can have an identity as a worker without losing their Indigenous identity.

This does not mean I completely agree with Howard Adams. In the mid-1970s when he was a mentor of mine, I learned a great deal from him. Howard aligned with development theory, which was theorized by economists such as Andre Gunder Frank and others who were looking at Latin America, the Caribbean, and Africa, and how European colonialism/capitalism underdeveloped these peoples. The United Nations decolonization mission adopted development theory, with formerly colonized nations calling for transfer of technology and wealth from the rich countries, a kind of reparations plan. The entire regime collapsed in 1980, when the United States withdrew its participation. Howard, like Coulthard, saw alternative Indigenous development as a way to undermine capitalism.

Howard Adams also linked US and Canadian overseas imperialisms as something not new to the twentieth century

---

15   The Métis, a people located mostly in the southern and central areas of Manitoba, had their origins in the mixed-race descendants of the First Nations people and early colonial British and French settlers. Louis David Riel was a nineteenth-century Métis who led two rebellions against the Canadian government and was executed in 1885.

but rooted in their colonization of the peoples of North America. He was a pioneer in making that connection in the early 1970s. Now, for Native scholars, it is taken for granted.

But it's not surprising that both Coulthard and Adams come out of the Indigenous communities in Canada, where they didn't experience the level of anti-communism that existed in the United States. The Communist Party in Canada early on included many of the First Peoples who organized Communist Party chapters, particularly in Native fishing villages in British Columbia. The Native presence in or near the Marxist left and trade unions is very different than in the United States.

However, I think a great many Native people in the United States very much feel a unity with militant workers' struggles. I've always found in the Native movement when I tell stories about my grandfather, about the history of the IWW and Socialist Party in Oklahoma, and especially about the 1917 Green Corn Rebellion, in which landless Native, Anglo, and African American tenant farmers rose up against conscription into World War I, calling it a "rich man's war," that there is a sense of hope and possibility for solidarity to struggle together in mutual interest.

Transcribed by Michelle Ward

Clifton Ariwakehte Nicholas

Anarchism and First Peoples — colonialism in its beginnings — nationalism and language — the reservation system — religion — difficult alliances — the warriors — political violence and its consequences — the military — Palestine, Greece, Chiapas

Clifton Nicholas is a Kanyen'kehà:ka activist, filmmaker, and entrepreneur from Kanesatake. He took part in the conflict known as the "Oka Crisis" following the blockade of Kanesatake by the Canadian army between July and September 1990. He made a few independent documentaries such as *Elsipogtog: No Fracking Way!* which addresses the Mik'maw resistance against fracking on their territory, as well as *Karistatsi Onienre: The Iron Snake* on the pipeline project called Énergie Est.

When did you first get in touch with anarchism? With books, people?

People. I think it was after 1990, probably 1998 or 1999. I used to go to school at Concordia University, in Montreal. That's when I met all these people.

When we interviewed Gord Hill, we were telling him about this word, anarcho-indigenism. He said that he didn't use the word because he said he thought what was important was anti-capitalism

and anti-colonialism. Do you know a lot of onkwehonwe people who would call themselves anarchists?

They wouldn't but they have anarchist tendencies. The lack of education (and the same thing goes in the white society) is what makes people think in a certain way. I try to educate whenever I can. Most of the time I piss people off in my community. This is what it is. I'm known as "the activist," but I don't give a shit. Again, you know the propaganda models that are put out by the media in the mainstream society, how they describe anarchism as a highly negative thing, when you mention anarchy, they think of total destabilization, everything's running havoc, like people killing each other in the streets or eating each other, that's what they think anarchy is. Then I say "well, I don't know, Noam Chomsky is an anarchist and this is what anarchism means" and then they say "oh you mean Gaianerekowa!" You know, anarchists have certain rules that we follow. I wouldn't say we're ruleless, and you go to most Mohawk communities, they reject the notion of having a leader. Even the ones who are capitalist in their tendencies and what they do, they reject this idea of having a leader. "He's not my leader, fuck, he's my cousin!", you know what I mean?

Unfortunately, due to capitalism and colonization, we tend to stop thinking in those terms, and start putting our so-called speakers and spokespersons who were called by a word that was mistranslated into chief, we put them up on a level like they're leaders but that's not how it is traditionnally. Like even the word "chief," we used a word that means "the good mind" (the same word exists for women). But even though they have anarchist tendencies in how they carry themselves, they do a lot of capitalist things. When you talk about a population that's been impoverished in colonization for the last two hundred years, when they're offered an opportunity to get wealth of any sort, it's hard to say to them "don't; no you don't want that big truck, no you don't want that big TV." Even myself, it's hard when you don't have anything, to go from nothing to something.

The first Europeans came here from very hierarchical societies (the priests, the barons, the chiefs ...). A lot of common folks discovered a new way of life and freedom. For the priests, for the elite, the word savage was a bad word, but for some common folks, it was a good word. To "become savage" in some French texts of the time, was to become free, to pass on the other side, to flee from European colonization and society and to go toward your people.

This is something that appeals a lot to anarchists. I think the anarchism of late is more and more opened to those ideas of recognizing the anarchist roots, they don't necesarily come from a white source. Your notion of individual freedom does not come from Europe, it comes from here. Because when they left Europe, the English, French, and German and Dutch settlers, they left a world of priests, barons, landlords, and kings. There was no such thing as individual freedom, no such thing as mobility between classes. You're a serf, you be a serf when you go to the New World. You're a blacksmith, you're gonna stay a blacksmith.

But there's also, in the native people, the thing of not eating the shit of the state, and defying, going against the apparatus of the state, because we do not recognize the state. Again it all went back to that initial contact period, coming from a very stratified society, based on wealth and keeping those who don't have in line, the feudal system they left ... So it became problematic when they sent the lower caste people, the common folk here to be workers and to settle. But they didn't send women, they sent men, common men to do the dirty work for the elite. If you look at "*le coureur des bois*," these voyageurs who said "fuck society, I'm gonna find an Indian woman, fall in love, and have children." They were the original smugglers, the original suppliers of illegal furs in the colony. And the fact is they stopped selling to the French and started selling to the Dutch and the British, it threatened the existence of this colony right here. So they had to call on and bring over those poor French women, *les "filles du Roy,"* to bolster the settlement here, so that men don't run away with Indian women. But sometimes, both men and women left with the Indians too! It was an issue because they didn't want to recognize that their society is causing this. People didn't want this society anymore, they saw freedom! A lot of white, French and English captives who were taken by my people back in the day, they were taken because part of our ceremonies is when you lose somebody, you have to replace them in the mourning ritual. After a certain period of time, they were given the right to leave. But 90 percent of them stayed. That's why in some places like Kahnawake, some families have those last names like William (those were captives from Massachusetts) for example, some families married with Irish as well (and the Irish were infamous because they came as slaves, with the black slaves, and they revolted, and that's why they invented the whole issue of being white and black, the invention of whiteness). A lot of native people were mixed with black as well ... the Seminole are quite well known for that. One of the main differences with the English and French, is that the English were very removed, they didn't wanna know or see, whereas the French would marry into the native societies and have families, especially here in Quebec. Thus it is a métis society in a lot of ways; today, a lot of people disregard that part of history. I think what gets me now in Quebec society is how some of that mainstream society got their hand so wrapped around those things like patrimony, France ... they tend to forget that France lost, and even got money out of it, so stop that fucking Charles de Gaulle-*vive-le-Québec-libre*

65

example. We have to bridge that gap. I wish that it was simpler and that I could speak Innu, but we're stuck with English or French.

I agree when they say they have to preserve the language. But I draw a line when they say preserve the language and tie it to a culture, tie it to whiteness, that's another issue.

Yet, we deal with a lot of racism in the community too, even against blacks. That's another thing I try to fight a lot. And I say we're under the same shitty end of the stick as the black community. I've been trying for some years to create a bridge with black communities. No white activists, just native and black, no offense. I just want to connect with them. There's so much that needs to be said. Because if we get together, that'd be fucking scary. But even then in the black community, they have a lot of issues too.

To speak about individual and collective identities, you know that over the last 20 years, the same thing has been popping up in the Quebec mainstream media, regarding Kahnawake residency rules. Those debates are rarely very smart and rarely very informed; most of the time, when people talk about that issue they seem to forget we're within a colonial context, which involves colonial structures such as the band council system. Could you tell us a bit more about that system?

You mean blood quantum residency I guess. That's totally colonial. That has nothing to do with traditional people in Kahnawake or here, who do not support those residency rules or this blood quantum bullshit. Because traditionally, if you were walking around our territory and we catch your ass back in the day, we brought you back to the village and eventually accepted you, you'd be brought to that ceremony that would be done after a period of time, we'd ask you if you wanted to be adopted and we would literally strip you naked in the middle of the village and have a bath and wash you. After you'd been washed, they'd dry you off, they'd take that water and say "now, who you were is gone, you're no longer Benjamin, you're whatever-name-they'd-give-you from this day on, we don't recognize you as anything other than one of us," you're Kanyen'kehà:ka now. In a way they were treated like slaves, no doubt although it was not the same type of chattel slavery the British, the French, and the Americans had.

However, on the political side of it, you'd never have an official voice, because you're adopted. Your children would as long as they have a clan. But you would never have a voice. But, you'd be able to stand up and say "this is what I think." You would have a voice as a pine tree representative, you'd be able to voice your opinion, you just wouldn't have an official voice to bring forward. That's something the band councils don't follow. If you look at that legislation they're going on, it's an Indian Act legislation that prevents white people to be in the community. It's a very destructive thing. And unfortunately, at Kahnawake they have their reasons: it's completely surrounded by urban setting, it's a little more insular than here.

I think one of the biggest problems we have as onkwehonwe people is the fact we're relegated to the reserves. We don't have any chance of mobility. Back in the day, before colonialism, we were able to get up, move, and start another village somewhere if we wanted to. People could split to mitigate issues. We can't do that anymore, we're stuck on the reserve. The reality is people don't necessarily always want to be with each other. Even now, white people are freer than we are; if you're not happy in Montreal, you can move somewhere else. It's not to say I can't, but I can't really go to another reserve because it's the same shit over there too. The lack of mobility stops a lot of issues from being resolved within this colonial system, pretty much by design.

On that same line of thought, regarding internal divisions, as a settler and as someone who lives and interacts with other anarchists, we see a lot of division within the anarchist community. These divisions tend to create what could be called ideological parochialism, divisions that have negative consequences (it's hard to build a movement, it's a waste of energy and so on). On the other hand, we see that onkwehonwe struggles are very diverse internally, ideologically speaking.

But it does. I think division is just part of the human condition. We do have very diverse ideologies, we have religious differences. I am myself an atheist, I don't follow religion, traditional or not. I'd support traditional teachings more than Christianity, mind you. I've got a really big issue with Christianity. I fucking despise it [chuckles]. I think that's the worst thing that ever happened to our people. 'Cause the most severe division that we have, the most severe setbacks come from that fucking Bible. All the time. It's used against us.

So yeah, religion fosters a lot of division within this community. And if you look at things through the lens of religion, you realize the people who support the most the band council system are Christians. They're the biggest adversaries of non-Christian traditionals, by large.

You're a big fan of metal; does it have anything to do with your political beliefs?

I think so, particularly some of the thrash metal I was listening to in the 1990s. Some of it is very politically left, such as Kreator. Like their song "Material World Paranoïa" for example. The lyrics go like "desperation in the factory, crank out oblivion, material world paranoïa, slavery begins at birth" stuff like that. That's pretty anarchistic right? Even a little bit of Slayer, like "Mandatory Suicide," songs like that always stuck in my head. I didn't just listen to the music, I learned the lyrics. It helped me feel comfortable in there but I wouldn't give it too much credit. Metal is pretty much an outsider music. Now not so much. Back then I used to do a metal show and the local preacher would call me up and threaten me for going to hell and all that.

To come back to anarcho-indigenism, we see this term coming up in the activist settler literature, as a way to say "here it is, there's a solidarity happening between anarchist and Indigenous struggles." Do you see that happening in Quebec?

I do see some bridges being made, but at the same time, there's never been total cooperation between the two. I think it's impossible because Indigenous people do not want that. It's a bit like Malcolm X said: you can be in solidarity, but you cannot be part of us. I think that a lot of—and it's not intended to anybody—non-Indigenous people involved in anarchism are trying to become part of it, they're feeling so alienated in this society coming from capitalism and colonization from Europe, so destructive of the individual that they wanna grasp at something more pure, more rich—I think there's this search of purity also in movements. But you look at Indigenous people, it's not a pure thing, it's a thing that's been damaged. We lost like 90 percent of our populations to war and disease ... how do you remain viable, all the minds, thinkers, inventors, medicine people ... we're still here but only as a vestige of what we were ...

Survivors?

Survivors for sure!

It is thus still hard for alliances?

I respect all the movements, but I think anarchism is still a white kinda thing, like people of color are still a minority within these kinds of movements. You know I use the term white, I hate that term, it's not necessarily about the complexion of your skin. There's white, and there's white as in "I'm the boss." So issues are usually approached through a white perspective, and there's this type of white knight syndrome. We don't want you to save us. That's an issue. But at the same time, not everyone does it. It's more acceptable now for anarchists to come to that community than what it used to be. Before it was more like "get these fuckers outta here." Now it's more like "oh they're your friends—yeah, they mean well, that's what they do" and anarchists see so many actions they can stand by. I myself call them allies, or rather accomplices. At the same time, I think you've got to tread very carefully and not just talk to the like-minded anarchistic Indigenous folks like myself. You know as much as I like some anarchists, sometimes I think "get easy guys, I don't like that, I don't want to be your token." I told them to find somebody else for a while, because I don't want to be the "native spokeperson" because I'm not. You've got to talk to other mainstream people in the community about their thoughts on the same issues. Many anarchists find it very confusing sometimes, because some people look at Indigenous people for utopias. Like, "look at those native people, they're just like I am, they think the same way," but it's not as simple as that. Indigenous folks for the most part have suffered a lot. So when they see that white skin, they identify it with oppression.

You've been a prominent Mohawk voice for quite a while now, particularly since the so-called Oka Crisis in 1990; you've been making movies, you've traveled around the world to speak about your experience, particularly about onkwehonwe struggles, you've even been harassed by the Canadian Security Intelligence Service

*(CSIS) because of this. How do you consider yourself? How would
you describe yourself to people who do not know you?*

Human being, and I think it falls in line with how we say it in
my language, "onkwehonwe," which means "human being." I
come to this point after many years of introspection; after the
crisis, I was a Mohawk-centrist, I didn't want to know nothing
about white people, I was very angry, and I think in some
regards rightfully so. But what helped me is I'm tri-lingual,
so I know a lot of people in the French community also, and
I know a lot of non-natives that were very angry and hurt by
what happened also, so that helped me get past those first three
years after the crisis and forming a different political ideology.

So I would describe myself as a human being now ... onkwehonwe, and we all share this same family. If we all strive to
be human beings and put away some of these things we put
ahead of everything else it will be a lot easier to get along in
the world and recognize the humanity in each other. Some
people try to ask me if I'm part of the warrior society; that's
ridiculous because it's not a formal structure. Every man's
responsibility is to be a warrior. Every woman's responsibility is to be a warrior. Then I would go further to say I'm a
Kanyen'kehà:ka. And that's part of being onkwehonwe; being
Kanyen'kehà:ka is being part of that, it's your responsibility,
your duty to stand up and defend what we need to defend.
A warrior is somebody who is community minded, being
somebody who will help people who need help; he has to be
selfless and it's not easy, even for myself, I'm not gonna say
I'm selfless because sometimes I do not fill the mold either.

A warrior encompasses much more than just holding a gun,
and this is the distinction between being an armed individual, bordering on thug, bordering on gangster, and being a
warrior. I don't hold a gun anymore, yet I still consider myself
a warrior. I use other weapons. The other ones are never too

far, mind you. But my choices are different because I think we have tools we need to use that were developped over the years that are more effective. There is a time and a place for everything.

We are glad you started talking about the warrior society because we also wanted to talk about it. For instance, during the so-called Oka Crisis, many settlers discovered the existence of the Mohawk Warrior Society, they had never really heard about it before. What is it exactly? How would you explain it?

What we know today since 1990 as the warrior society has its roots in the early 1970s and late 1960s. We've always had a warrior movement, a warrior society within our culture prior to contact. It went somewhat dormant after the war of 1812[1] because we suffered a great deal after that war. The war of 1812 was like the death knell for those warriors of that era because we were ravaged by disease, ethnic cleansing in New York State. They physically removed us, forced us in just the same way you saw the ethnic cleansing after Bosnia and Herzegovina, the same thing happened to us, just like the ethnic cleansing that happens in Palestine. After 1812, this is when we started being relegated to reserves, this is where our children started being abducted, taken into schools. And then the advent of the Indian Act in 1876[2] was again an extension of that. So for a long time, I was there but it lay very dormant,

---

1   The war of 1812—in which the Mohawk took part, on the side of the British—opposed the young United States to Canada (which at the time was still a British dominion).

2   *The Canadian Encyclopedia* website: "The Indian Act is the principal law through which the federal government administers Indian status, local First Nations governments and the management of reserve land and communal monies. ... The Act came into power on 12 April 1876. It consolidated a number of earlier colonial laws that sought to control and assimilate Indigenous peoples into Euro-Canadian culture."

it wasn't active and organized. In the 1960s, not only in the black cultures but also in the Indigenous cultures, and in most segments of the oppressed, there was a movement, a rising of the tides. You look at the civil rights movements in the 1960s where a lot of the Indigenous people who were forced out of their territories into the cities, they were looking for something to get through to the creation of the American Indian Movement in the urban centers. And it spread out more into the rule-settings of the reserves after the 1970s; and the warrior movements too, our warrior movement also started up under traditional guidelines and how we maintained our warriors through the Kaianerekowa and our traditions; they became more viable at that point. I think the first act of the warrior movement was the taking over of land in New York State. You know there's a girls' camp in New York State [near Old Forge, at Moss Lake] and they took it over and the first Kanyen'ke-hà:ka settlement was there (in my language, Kanyenke is the territory, Kanyen'kehà:ka is the people and Kanyenkeha is the language, it's all based on that root, "Kanyenke"). There was a lot of gunfire and battles with locals and the police and it finally settled at Ganienkeh where it is today near Altona, New York. It was a right of return, you could say, just like the Palestinians are trying to have. That's what we exercised, and we established that. So it's a territory in New York State that's totally independent, there's no federal subsidies or anything; it stands and it's sovereign territory. And the name Ganienkeh means Mohawk territory, Mohawk nation.

So that movement really started getting more organized with the advent of the unity flag, a.k.a. the warrior flag, and a lot of the art and writing of Louis Hall started coming out in the early 1970s and through to the 1980s. It started developing itself more in the 1980s, and there was the influx of cigarettes at that time too in the mid- to late 1980s and they grew from there using it as a funding source to buy radio equipment, to organize, and we had the first real hard confrontation with the Royal Canadian Mounted Police (RCMP) in 1988 during a police raid in Kahnawake against the cigarette stores. That was the first time we blocked the Mercier bridge, for 24 hours. Then 1990 occurred. But before that, we had this little war alone with ourselves. In Akwesasne, there was a shooting happening within ourselves; we had a pro-gambling faction and an anti-gambling faction and, unfortunately, some people who were claiming to be part of the warrior society were on the pro-gambling side of things and those who weren't were on the anti-gambling side. I'm not going to go into detail that much about it because I don't like to talk about it with non-onkwehonwe people, but it was a serious issue, two men were murdered at the end of the conflict, they were shot to death, houses were burned, and there's still a lot of pain from that.

Then 1990 happened. I find it repugnant what happened in Akwesasne on all sides because we have that Gaianerekowa, which was designed to foster peace among ourselves and that's why it's called in English "the great law of peace." It's by no means a pacifist thing. We buried our weapons against each other, but that doesn't mean we buried our weapons against external threats. And history shows we never did that, if you look at the Gaianerekowa being ratified in the 1100, and there's a period between 1100 to 1812 when we did a lot of fighting. But there is always that dialogue that needs to happen before you fight. The dialogue, if you can foster peace, you foster it, if you can't, you can't.

What about the women within the warrior society? Do they play a specific role, or have a specific influence particularly within Mohawk culture?

They have a significant role, there is no warrior society without women. The original warrior flag has a woman and a man on it, a man side by side with a woman and they both have one feather in their head, which means they're both one mind, they have to share the same mind. In our traditions, the title holders of the land are the women, the lineage goes through the women. The Earth is a feminine thing and we look at warfare also in that manner. The men will fight the wars but the women will call upon the men to do the duties they have to do. It's not a male decision per se. This is the confusion I've tried to explain to feminists as well: yes women are in charge, but it's egalitarian. We're not gonna jump from matriarchy to patriarchy or vice versa, it's egalitarian. We're very balanced. Women had certain duties to do things like say, call war. They would call it, it would be their final decision to make, and once that decision was made, they would bury the fires so there would be no hearth to go back to. It's the men's decision at that point. Women didn't have tactical input. They were allowed to fight but only after men would have been exhausted. There are certain rules, certain things. You have the decision-making process, the war-making process, and the reason why women have that role is also because women debrief the men when they come back, they're the ones who take away that trauma, all the things that we neglected.

Whether you're being an anarchist or Black Bloc type of thing, there's the need for debrief after because whenever you engage in a violent act, you also need to disengage. You look at all these vets, they come back and they have what they call post-traumatic stress disorder (PTSD). In our ways, when the men go to war, they don't even have the right to enter the village until they've gone through the ceremony that brings them back and cleanses their minds. They take care of mental wounds.

Maybe you could tell us about the impact of violence on the community. Kanehsatake and Kahnawake have suffered from the aftermath of the use of violence, because of police repression and brutality that came because of the tools and methods the communities used effectively. That's the thing I'd be interested to hear you about.

Of the saddest things that happened because of the use of violence—and this is the problem with violence, especially when you're in an oppressed community like ours—is that violence went to a certain level, and when people didn't agree, the violence turned in on the same community, and we suffered within ourselves. And it's hard sometimes when we externalize the violence and it comes back and it internalizes itself. And that's the dangerous part of it.

And do women play a role in this?

Yeah, they have a central role in this, they're the ones taking care of the ceremony, they're the ones who help you bring your mind back. Like I said, it's very egalitarian. There's a recognition of the feminine way of thinking. As men, we tend to be more rash; if I push you right away, you're gonna push me back. Whereas a woman considers things differently. I'm generalizing but for the most part, instead of being so reactionary, women will think harder about different actions before men will. They consider things differently. When men will even forget they're fathers, they'll forget the kids and they'll react. But what happens after? What if you get hurt? Who's gonna take care of you after?

Also, like my mom says—and my mom is very anti-warfare—you know when you bring up a child, she says, I cannot imagine sending my kid to go and die. That's the logic.

In videos about the warrior society, sometimes we can see women wearing the outfit and being on the barricade with the guys, so I guess it's possible too?

Yeah, for sure, it is. But you know, and I might sound misogynistic, but when the men are on the line, someone has to feed them. Somebody has to take care of them. One of the things I try to talk about with people—because it's hard to fight my masculine identity and my misogynistic way of thinking sometimes, like "it's a man job" or criticizing a man because he's afraid to be on the frontline; well then, we'll give him a different role, he doesn't have to get on the frontline. In 1990, a couple of guys, they got so scared, they fled. We were pretty hard on them, and I should not have done that, I should have been softer with them, a little more understanding.

Taiaiake Alfred was part of the Marines, Gord Hill was in the army reserve, you said you considered going into the army at some point. Is there a pattern here? Hence why we wonder; we saw a lot of young Indigenous guys going into the army, does that have something to do with cultural traits?

I think a lot of young men just want that adventure. That's what I wanted. I don't think that was any sort of ancient calling, with the eagle and all that [chuckles] calling me to join and kill people ... That's no part of the warrior tradition, that's just about young guys full of testosterone who get to shoot guns. So when I was a kid, I just liked that type of thing, I played with soldier models, that's just it! Don't over analyze it.

Yet, my granduncle was probably partly responsible for that, putting all his medals on for Remembrance ... I never made the jump between him putting on his medals, standing all proud of what he did, and then getting totally fucking drunk that night, drinking with all the other vets and not being in a good place. When you're young you just don't think about it, but you get destroyed the older you get. And you realize it when they start sharing their stories. And you start thinking "Man … that's why you're drinking." I'd be drinking too! He told stories of being so scared and being trapped under a porch in a little hamlet in France on their way to Caen for days because the Germans were all over. So living a fear like that and coming back to a place when they had nothing. All the other veterans they fought with they got bursaries to go to school, they had job opportunities, but not him. They gave him like 50,000 dollars when he was 92. He said "I'm dead, I'll be dead in a few years, what the hell am I gonna do with all this money?"

For a while the Canadian state had a policy of trying to get as many Indigenous people as possible in the army … They still do, but at a point in history, you had the right to vote if you were a veteran.

That's part of the assimilation process. They want to remove as many of us as they can. They want to integrate everybody so that the land issue can disappear. The same thing worked with education. If you went to post-secondary education, you'd become disenfranchised. You weren't allowed to come back. So in other words, if you became educated—let's say I became a lawyer—I wasn't allowed to come back to defend my people, stuff like that.

You know, many anarchists would find really problematic this flirt with the military, among the Native youth.

That's actually one thing that bothers me with anarchists when they talk about non-conformity. Fuck off man, you want me to conform big time, you know what I mean? I do my thing, I work with a lot of anarchists, I consider myself that in some ways (in some ways I don't), but like I said in the beginning, I consider myself a human being. And as a human being I have many facets. I try to always be conscious about what I do, what I choose, and why I choose it.

I like the anarchist movement, but sometimes I feel they're over-critical and it gets to me sometimes. I think that's what causes a lot of divisions in the movement, that over-criticizing of things and of ourselves.

The reason we were asking you about the warrior society is because a lot of anarchists look at it and they're quite impressed by what they see, like Elsipotog,³ the Oka Crisis, it just seems to speak to a lot of anarchists. Do you think there is something similar between the warrior society and anarchism?

Yes and no. If you look at our people, our people tend to be very individualistic, they don't like to be kind, they don't like to be led. It can be a pro and a con sometimes. I'll repeat a quote from the Jesuits' Relations that says in the very distasteful way it was written "these Iroquois, they have no masters, no gods, they follow no one, they're sovereign unto themselves," which I think is awesome, it's a great thing! And that's how my people are, in a lot of ways.

But if you're talking about a tactical edge, discipline is a very important thing when you're fighting, being able to give and take orders and do things like that in that situation, that can be very difficult.

Anarchists have been accused of violence by mainstream society (the window-smashing argument is quite well

---

3   In 2013, in the Canadian province of New Brunswick, the Mi'kmaq organized a blockade against oil companies and set fire to many police vehicles.

known); the Mohawks have been accused of pretty much the same thing by Quebec's mainstream society (blockading and all that stuff). Anarchists usually reject the argument of window smashing either by advocating violence against the state (one can't really call their behavior violent when it's only about resisting and freeing oneself, compared to the state that uses violence to oppress). As a Mohawk, what would be your answer to those accusations of violence?

Yes, we've been accused of violence. But it's kind of a tricky thing to answer and it's not something I necessarily like to talk about too often, outside of certain circles, 'cause I just don't really know you, you know? I'll talk about it with my brethren … And I think that's what confuses many young people in this community, that we're gonna play this tactic all the time. And that becomes redundant after a while, and ineffective.

Yet, there's a time and place for everything. I think we use violence in a necessary time and place. As for violence, I'm not a pacifist in any way but at the same time I'm not someone who's gonna go for gratuitous violence just for the sake of violence. And sometimes I find that some demos are just gratuitous. I understand frustration, but at the same time I think there are other tactics.

I think as a movement, we have to consider too that we'll never outrun the state. Never. That's fucking bullshit. Illusion. Even though I know places in Kahnawake and here that are heavily armed. There's a reason why the SQ [Sûreté du Québec], when they do an intervention here, they come in armored vehicles because they know too. They hear it, like at New Year's Eve, there's a lot of automatic gunfire going off. They're not stupid. But that multiplies itself. That makes the responses that more dangerous. And everytime they do interventions, they bring those armored vehicles and heavy guns, it ups the chance that people are getting killed. And that, to me, especially as a Mohawk, there are not many of us. So that each person that would die in a confrontation, it is an extreme tragedy. Native people are so few compared to the general society, it does have a great impact.

A lot of anarchists claim the use of violence is legitimate but seldom manage to use it as a way that's actually threatening to the State.

They don't use it effectively. One thing that I'm totally against is kettling. I find it ridiculous that we allow ourselves to be kettled at demos. That's why I don't go to demos in Montreal, because I won't allow myself to be kettled. It's one thing to march, it's important to march, but it's also important to be tactical and take it to another level. I think that the mainstream society here in Quebec has not suffered enough to be ready to take it to a violent level. The time I spent in Greece, the cops won't even dare get close to the demos, because the anarchists and the communists will attack them. I loved it over there. And I felt at home. Not to say there aren't things that are problematic also.

That was actually the point of our next question. We remember when the CSIS called you regarding your trip to Greece, on the recording of the call they ask you at some point about how you reconcile your Mohawk roots and your anarchist activism. You didn't want to respond to them, right?

What I wanted to say to him when he asked that is "how do you reconcile being a human being and working for such a bastard organization? Can you explain that to me, I'll explain you the other one!" [laughter]. It's important to remain silent. Because everytime you give them a modicum of information, they use that to profile you.

It's a tool they use. All activists, especially anarchists, have to remember that. Don't say anything. And it's getting precarious right now because they basically created the legislation that gives the police more powers. So now it's gonna become very scary. So when they do call you, you'll be obligated. So don't give them anything. I don't want to talk to them about what I did in 1990. They already know.

So, in line with your trip to Greece, how do you relate Indigenous struggles to other social or political movements in the world, like let's say the Greek anarchists fighting against their state, or the apartheid in Palestine?

What you're looking at in Palestine is still the initial phases of colonization. It's only about 70 years of colonization over there, whereas here it's about 350 to 500 years. And the population numbers are much greater, they don't have to contend with virulent diseases the way we did. So there are differences. Regarding Greece, I couldn't relate in terms of being an Indigenous person to them because there is no real Indigenous person, it's their own people doing it to them. So I'd have to relate to it almost as a band council situation and a band council doing things to us. It was harder for me to make that connection.

So you were there in 2013?

Yeah, I was there for over a month.

So the movement is pretty big there, right?

It's huge! It's actually a threat. The police and the military treat it as a threat. But again, Greece is a very weird situation, it's something I'm not necessarily comfortable commenting on too much because I only touched on that for a very brief period. But what I did see was interesting. Because it's very integrating. You have older people, lots of them, working there, they fill the void left by the state due to austerity. And you see a lot of people from different segments of the society there. It's not to say there's not the more radical anarchists, like the Black Bloc type of anarchists.

What about Latin America?

What about it?

In 1994, when the Zapatistas made their move, many anarchists in Europe for instance believed it was a big thing, that it was very interesting, and that it was—in a way—anarchistic, with general assemblies, civilian power over the military, yet so different from the Marxist-Leninist type of guerilla that went through the 1960s. Do you see any link with them, do you follow what happens there?

I follow it but I don't have a direct link. I know some people in our traditional government had gone there and have communications with them. We support them, they support us. I think it was inspiring to see that happening after 1990, because it was right after. Also the speeches made, the famous sub-commandant Marcos statement: "Marcos is gay in San Francisco, black in South Africa, a Mohawk in Quebec … " : we're in that speech! It's the same thing for me, I'm a Zapatista in Chiapas. And even then, when I talk about Turtle Island, my Turtle Island ends at Tierra del Fuego. It starts up north at the North Pole and goes all the way down to Tierra del Fuego.

Véronique Hébert[1]

Anarchist theater — kids — words that do not exist — what is anarchism? — indigeneity in the Americas — the Polytechnique massacre and the Oka Crisis — women and feminism — spirituality — colonialism and decolonialism — cultural blending and *métissage*

Véronique Hébert is a Quebecois Métis from the Atikamekw First Nation of Wemotaci. She was born in La Macaza where her mother was studying at Manitou College, a school for Indigenous leaders. Véronique studied theater at various educational institutions where she put on numerous theatrical creations, including a version of Samuel Beckett's *Waiting for Godot* at the Sudbury Theatre Festival in Ontario in 2011; *Les mots qui n'éxistent pas* (literally "words that do not exist"), a feminist political discourse in conjunction with theater artist Pol Pelletier; and *MatinSoir*, a comic reflection on the role of culture and mythology in Indigenous relations with non-Indigenous people, presented at the First Nations Garden in Montreal in 2014. She wrote, directed and acted in collective theatrical works with Atikamekw youth and professional artists for the festival Présence Autochtone in Montreal from 2013 to 2015. She also created a personal original work called *Métusse*, which was presented at the Printemps autochtone d'art in 2013. Inspired by the story of Antigone from Greek mythology, it addresses social justice and Indige-

---

1   Translated by Ellen Warkentin.

nous rights through a feminist lens.[2] She has repeatedly put on political theater with a musical component for the festival Présence Autochtone, staging young actors into a chorus similar to those in ancient Greek theater. While seeking inspiration from European theater traditions, she also promotes openness toward other Indigenous nations: "These borders [imposed by colonization] are neither ours nor those of nature […]. That's why we must symbolically open the borders in order to develop real ties uniting and unifying all First Nations." She emphasizes the importance of "drawing from Indigenous movements that continue to maintain their culture elsewhere on the planet."[3]

You staged a play called Les mots qui n'existent pas *(The words that don't exist) at both the Présence Autochtone Festival and the Montreal Anarchist Theatre Festival.*

It was the playwright and actress Pol Pelletier who first suggested producing a play for the Anarchist Theatre Festival. I put it on with other actors, including my eight-year-old daughter, but Pol and I wrote the script.

How did you react to the initial suggestion? Were you already familiar with anarchists and anarchism?

I didn't have a clear idea, but of course I knew that anarchists were involved in resistance movements and that they didn't recognize governmental authority. I was happy to partici-

---

2   www.montheatre.qc.ca/espace/2013/04/29/printemps-autochtone-dart-relier-les-racines-et-la-contemporaneite/.

3   Isabelle L'Héritier, "Se regrouper pour faire rayonner l'art autochtone," *Alternatives*, December 4, 2013 (http://journal.alternatives.ca/spip.php?article7628). See also: Véronique Hébert, "Le théâtre autochtone: un parcours entre pratique et théorie," Jérôme Dubois and Dalie Giroux (eds.), *Les arts performatifs et spectaculaires des Premières nations de l'Est du Canada* (Paris: L'Harmattan, 2014).

pate in a festival that promoted and practiced decentralized methods of making art: art with a small budget, created right next to its audience. As an Indigenous woman and a feminist, the only places available to me are at the margins of the theater community. Staging one of my plays at the Anarchist Festival seemed more worthwhile and relevant than putting it on at the Théâtre du Nouveau Monde. I prefer making symbolic statements to working with official institutions, and I often refuse to present scripts at official events. In any case, art is a psycho-magical power that has its own force.

In the play Les mots qui n'existent pas, *the character who represents your daughter asks: "Mom, what is anarchism?"*

Yes, that's a reference to the concept of anarchism as a refusal to recognize authority. My daughter is an anarchist by her very nature; all children are, really, as a result of their pure freedom. Anarchism taps into the very essence of childhood. As a mother, I manage my daughter's anarchism on a daily basis! And I do it through negotiation, not through repression. As a parent, I've almost always been against homework. It is presented as necessary to acquire academic knowledge and therefore mandatory for academic success. That very fact makes academic assessment unfair, because not every parent can help their children with homework. Success is therefore influenced by whether or not you belong to a certain social class or group. For example, new immigrants or illiterate people can't contribute to the "success" of their children. And especially in primary school, marks aren't even that important. My daughter should be able to ask questions about and be interested in things that are not covered by her academic education. I've always been a person who likes to question the system, and it seems absurd to me to make these young children follow all these rules, like waiting for the bell to ring to go to the bathroom or to drink some water, and then everyone has to go at once. Paradoxically, as adults, we're told to listen to our bodies and to try and find our "inner children." I think that's something that children can teach us. In my plays, I don't hesitate to send authority figures packing. Especially when they represent the patriarchy, like the police chief and the priest.

In Les mots qui n'existent pas, *you state that there are no words for "freedom" and "justice" in Atikamekw. Instead, you say that "Freedom is when the sun shines, when the bees fly with the birds above our heads in the sky."[4] Atikamekw technolinguists have created an Atikamekw word for "justice," to allow Indigenous peoples involved in the legal system to put their experience into words. From an anarchist perspective, it seems strange that a language would not have a word to express the concepts of freedom and justice.*

I have found no trace of these philosophical concepts in my language. They are understood or felt in a different way. I am interested in the contrasts between Atikamekw words, which try to convey a reality transformed by colonial powers, and the words these same colonial powers use to discuss similar concepts. I'm not a language specialist, but I find it very interesting, politically speaking, that the first Atikamekw neologisms created to describe colonial systems are related to loss, distress, violence, and suffering. These neologisms convey a loss of freedom by people subjected to the justice system, but they don't have anything to do with justice itself. Colonialism brought the abstract concepts of freedom and

---

4   Jasmyne Hébert, excerpt from the play *Les mots qui n'existent pas*, read during the National Aboriginal Day at Place Jacques-Cartier in Montreal, June 21, 2013.

justice along with it. However, the loss of real freedom and justice among Indigenous people is essentially tied to the colonialist justice system.

In the process of creating the play Les mots qui n'existent pas, *you talked to your mother, who worked all her life as an interpreter for the Atikamekw nation and for the federal Department of Justice, about the meaning of the word* violence. *It's a word that exists in Atikamekw, but you've said that it's a verb, an action. Can you tell us what that means, in political terms?*

Originally, in Atikamekw, violence was not an abstract concept, but rather an act expressed through action verbs like *beat* and *hit*. The abstract idea had to be invented. As an intergenerational repercussion of residential schools, I didn't grow up speaking my Indigenous language. I'm just learning Atikamekw now, and I practice it often. I'm no expert in the language, but I have observed my mother as she worked, and I can tell you that the non-Indigenous justice system has had a huge impact on the Atikamekw people. When the colonists first came over, how did their imported justice system affect the rights of First Nations people? How did it affect the way that land ownership and land use were negotiated? I can hardly bear to think about it. It seems completely absurd to me! I don't know if there's a word in Atikamekw for "absurd," but I really want to find out.

In the play Les mots qui n'existent pas, *one of the characters defines anarchy as the absence of power, but also as a kind of multiplicity in the face of a supposed unity. Do you think that pluralism is an important aspect of anarchy?*

In Indigenous communities, there are different cultures, different languages, different lands, different talents within a group. It's the diversity of anarchy. The Indigenous peoples of the Americas formed an immense civilization with various cultures that communicated with each other. When we go to the land of another Indigenous group, we establish relationships and discover common histories, because we share a common truth. Much has been erased, but this truth comes out when you trust the land to carry it, because the truth remains in the living land. The different Indigenous cultures visited each other, even when it took years. I realized that when I went to the Museum of Anthropology in Mexico City, where I saw that Algonquian (the language family that includes Atikamekw) was one of the pre-Hispanic languages of northern Mexico. So I learned that Indigenous languages traveled. One of my plays, *Oka*, is about this discovery.

In Mexico, Indigenous communities established dynasties. It was different here, where people were organized in small, autonomous, semi-nomadic groups that survived more or less by themselves. That's what it means, I think, to be an anarchist: doing what you need to do in order to get or achieve what you want. And that's also how I conceive of the ancestral ways of the Atikamekw. The idea of constantly rediscovering the land, of not taking it for granted. The idea of a freedom that is not named, because it is based on the living land. There is still so much shared by the Indigenous peoples of the Americas, even today. For example, the Oka Crisis in 1990 looked a lot like the Zapatista uprising that took place four years later. In both cases, the Indigenous rebels wanted to protect their land. In both cases, the rebels wore masks. The Zapatistas said, "We cover our faces so people will see us." The Mohawk warriors who defended their ancestral pine forests four years earlier seemed to have a certain influence on the Zapatistas. The similarities are undeniable. Interestingly enough, Mexico actually has the widest variety of pine species. Pines are very closely linked to Indigenous culture in Chiapas. And so the land unites us, both physically and symbolically.

We were surprised by the strong connection you establish in your work between the Montreal Massacre at the École Polytechnique on December 6, 1989, and the Oka Crisis that happened a few months later. You make this somewhat radical connection in the play Oka, *when a character says,*

> *You're wrong, Chief; the Oka Crisis is a response to the Polytechnique murders. Subconsciously, the Mohawks were reacting to the massacre of 14 young women, because they're living in a matriarchal society, they're the great builders of skyscrapers and steel. Women engineers, warrior builders. Ring a bell, Chief? École Polytechnique, December 6, 1989, an antifeminist shot down 14 women engineering students. Quebec is in a state of shock. Seven months later, right next to Montreal, the Mohawk communities of Kanesatake, Kahnawake and Akwesasne rise up and show Canada their great outrage. The Mohawk resistance was about more than standing up to people who want to enlarge their golf course. The Oka pine forest, which contained an ancestral burial ground, was the voice of our Outrage. We the First Nations, without even knowing it, we've started waking up. In our guts, something like a huge feathered serpent is growling. Queltzalcoatl, the feathered serpent. Queltzalcoatl, the Toltec god, the Aztec god [...] has wrapped his snake-like body around our spines.*

How did you draw the connection between the two events?

The killing at the École Polytechnique had a huge impact on my teenage years, both as a woman and as an Indigenous person living off the reserve. I was 13 or 14 years old when it happened, and it was swiftly followed by the Oka Crisis. As they both took place in the same area and time period, the two are inextricably linked in my adult mind. I also participated in a performance with Pol Pelletier of 14 repatriated women at the Sainte-Brigide-de-Kildare Church, a presentation in memory of the Polytechnique victims. I saw these women, they had enormous spirits. That's what happens when these kinds of tragedies happen in a specific territory, they have an impact on the collective subconscious. I was filled with that memory. The next year, on December 6, 2013, I made an offering at the foot of the monument at the École Polytechnique, and then I went to the Oka pine forest, where the barricades had been. I made an offering, and I heard a voice out of nowhere that said "Ho!" That voice came from the tall, majestic pine, a tree that grows both in North America and in Mexico. It was the same "Ho!" that is said at the end of certain prayers or speeches. I felt that I had entered into a sacred dialogue. All I had to do was to consciously make the connection, a connection of consciousness. Like I say in the play, the women who were killed at the Polytechnique would have become engineers, while the Mohawks had been the builders of bridges and skyscrapers in Quebec and in New York because they weren't afraid of heights. And the Mohawks traditionally lived in a matrilineal society, where the power of women was very strong.

And yet the image of the Warrior Mohawk wasn't very feminine during the Oka Crisis.

No. But the spokesperson, Ellen Gabriel, was a young woman who is still an activist today, advocating for the rights of women and Indigenous people. She'd been chosen by the elders to be a spokesperson for the movement.

Do you consider yourself a feminist?

At first, I thought that my difficulties in life were caused by the fact that I was Indigenous. Then, in my thirties, I discovered that in truth, it was because I am a woman. It took a long time before I could become a woman, I mean, an Indigenous woman. Being an Indigenous woman is twice as difficult, because you embody two converging political realities. Women are also considered a "minority" in a way, and our struggle is motivated by the need for personal and collective security. So I became a feminist. Because no one is born a feminist, you must choose to become one.

Did your new feminist identity cause friction within the Indigenous community?

That's still a delicate subject. What happened was that I took some workshops with Pol Pelletier and discovered all the women who played important roles throughout the history of theater. That's when I understood that I was a woman, and what it meant to be a woman. I realized that I had put aside my identity as a woman because I thought that the Indigenous struggle was more important than anything else. That's what I believed. In one way, I'm lucky that I chose to go into theater, because it allows me to express myself in a context where I can combine fiction and history. Today, I call myself a woman and a feminist Indigenous artist. I also see myself as a rebel. And I write about these things too. For example, the name of my play, *Métusse*, refers to a character who's a true rebel and who challenges the institutions that control her people.

But it took me a long time to call myself a feminist, maybe because feminism is still something remote for and misunderstood by Indigenous people. Not many Indigenous women call themselves feminists. They find that word to be heavy with history, especially after the Polytechnique massacre. And women also fear that feminism will divide or dilute the strength of the Indigenous struggle. I think that Indigenous women are reluctant to call themselves feminists because that might imply that they are abandoning Indigenous men, who are also struggling against the system for their own rights. They want to stand together, so they have to face both struggles at once. Maybe they will define themselves with a word that doesn't yet exist, a word that also encompasses the struggle against colonialism. The Native Women's Association was founded to defend the rights of Indigenous women who lost their Indian status if, for example, they married a white man. And yet a white woman would gain Indian status if she married an aboriginal man, so she could teach white culture and language to Indians. That's the incredibly racist and assimilationist government policy that was the driving force behind that women's movement.

And within the Indigenous community?

If I ask people I know, it seems as though most Indigenous women have a hard time calling themselves feminists even today. Even Eva Ottawa, former Grand Chief, mitigated the word, calling herself a "natural feminist," because she made the connection between feminism and Indigenous traditions. I also feel that there is a connection that must be made between feminism and anarcho-indigenism, in view of the strong traditional involvement of Indigenous women in the social sphere. I wasn't there, so I can't say for sure, but historically, it seems as though the equality and complementarity between women and men was greater, and equal value was placed on their respective social roles. In my personal experience, the place of women in the Atikamekw family and in the spiritual sphere seems more pronounced. I don't think any one culture or family type is perfect, but in the future, women will be taking up more space on all fronts and in all cultures ... Or at least, that is my hope!

Many Indigenous people hold the opinion that the roles of women and men should be complementary, but not necessarily equal.

In our spiritual teachings, we hold that each person has their own important role within a group. Each person has a talent, just as each species has its own colors and natural characteristics. Even the smallest plant can save your life. Complementarity also means respect and dignity, it means understanding the importance of every living creature. Unfortunately, as a result of colonialism (and now decolonialism as well), the Indigenous political space is in constant upheaval, looking for a balance between modernity and tradition. Colonization has changed our social fabric, our social roles. Indigenous men and women have tried to adapt to a political model and a way of life that does not correspond to their traditions, their experience or their reality. And we can't forget that colonization was a masculine venture. It was European men, not European women, who came to take control of the land, exploit resources, and establish trade relations. Men controlled the European colonial powers, and these same men were in positions of power in the colonies. So colonization imposed a system controlled by men, from which women were excluded from positions of power, and that clearly influenced relations between Indigenous men and women. I imagine that one of the effects of this power shift in the Indigenous community was that Indigenous men were involved in treaty negotiations, thinking that they had to protect the women.

The older generation of Atikamekw political leaders has had a hard time accepting the idea of women in power. Their conception of power was masculine and masculinist as a result of the colonial model. And we're still feeling those impacts

today. In my community, there's space for women to participate, but they often perform administrative tasks instead of
occupying the roles of chief, of advisor, of negotiator. As far
back as I can remember, most of the band council's administrative work was done by women, while the positions of power
were taken by men. But things are getting better. Eva Ottawa,
the Grand Chief of the Atikamekw nation, stepped down
because she wasn't being respected by the male chiefs. They
didn't recognize her authority. Clearly, feminism hasn't had
the desired positive influence in Indigenous political spheres.
We struggle against the effects of colonialism, but we forget
to adapt and advance and use the positive elements that the
rest of the world provides, because we're traumatized by our
experience with colonialism. Eventually, the men in our communities will have to step up and stop giving false excuses,
like when they claim that women don't traditionally have
any political experience. We have to start from scratch. One
day we'll have to have a conversation about why my mother
couldn't have been elected council chief, or even Grand Chief
of the Atikamekw nation. And maybe one day we'll have a
new food policy or a new agricultural policy, because for the
moment, I can't see how we can be self-sustaining. I mostly
see how we're leaving future generations to fend for themselves without any tools to be independent.

*And yet from the outside, it seems as though women are at the fore-
front of the Indigenous struggle. Is it an illusion?*

You have to realize that there's a difference between Indigenous rights advocacy movements and band council politics,
where you'll mostly see men in positions of power. It's not
surprising that Atikamekw women are the ones taking to the
streets to protest: they're excluded from all the places where
decisions are made. And yet despite all this, women are there,

doing the administrative tasks for the band council, teaching our youth, taking care of the community.

Furthermore, women have been throwing their weight around outside the traditional Canadian political system with movements like Idle No More, which I respect a lot, although I think it's too bad that there was no consultation with the communities. The media jump on certain individuals and see them as spokespeople for all Indigenous people, but in reality, they don't represent the reality of what is happening in many of our communities. And if you're not on Facebook, as is the case for many elders, you're not really being kept informed of the protests. That's another example of the changes that are happening in terms of power relations, changing the reality of political protest. I refuse to start a profile on Facebook, because then everything becomes virtual, even the relationships between us. I prefer to get the news late rather than rely on that kind of tool. Maybe I'm wrong, but I'm ready to take that risk, to take complete responsibility for it.

If you ask me, some movements and protests can do more harm than good because they draw attention away from the real issues without really making an impact outside of the virtual world. I have the feeling, and I hope I'm wrong, that people—Indigenous people included—take to the streets in protest, and then everyone just goes home and assumes that they've done their duty; they have nothing to feel guilty about so can go back to living within the established system. It's as though the goal of the protest is simply raising visibility, but no one cares if any real changes are made. This kind of mindset is dangerous for both politics and culture, because our protests are turning into spectacles. And once we've entered that territory, it's hard to get out again. I hardly ever go to protests. I'd rather write. That's my way of expressing my dissent. It's less ephemeral, more engaging.

You use the terms "colonialism" and "decolonization." What do these words mean to you in the present context? Do they describe two different realities?

I think that decolonization is an ideological movement that attempts to recreate the framework of a society before it was colonized. But it's impossible; it's like trying to walk backward under a ladder in an attempt to undo an evil hex. It's the same idea, just the opposite direction. We should be moving forward and forming new cultural, political, and social perspectives. We need to ally ourselves with other Indigenous and non-Indigenous groups. We need to regroup the Americas.

Your writings are imbued with spirituality. For example, in your interpretation of the play Waiting for Godot *at the Festival Théâtre Action in Sudbury in 2011, you wanted to explore the concepts of animism [the belief among Indigenous cultures that all things have a spirit and a soul, including animals, plants, and natural elements] and totemism [the act of forming an alliance with an animal or a plant, or recognizing it as the ancestor of a clan] and relate them to the ways in which our ancestors are responsible for the memory of the world and of the community. The European anarchist tradition harbors great mistrust toward religion, faith, and spirituality in general. This often comes across as a categorical rejection of any expression of faith. French anarchists have been known to express violence toward hijab-wearing Muslim women, as they see the hijab as a sign of oppression. But in doing so, anarchists are paradoxically stigmatizing these women that they see as oppressed. And the idea of the land being the guardian of memory … many anarchists see even that as too spiritual for their tastes.*

Anarchism is also about recognizing the plurality of perspectives, and not simply promoting a single hegemonic worldview. In the past, I often called Indigenous traditions into question as well. I thought these traditions were keeping me in the past, preventing me from moving forward. I was scared to challenge them, but I couldn't help but question certain aspects of the traditional ceremonies. And my perspectives were shocking to some of my older friends. But I eventually came to understand that tradition is simply a continuation of our relationship with our surroundings and with other people. Indigenous philosophy is based on ecology, but also on equality and justice. As we were semi-nomadic people, we developed values whereby our decisions were made by the group; the power wasn't in the hands of a single chief. We had to live with the land, and the land was also a source of danger. If you identify as Indigenous, you have to face the question of tradition: Where is your land? What is your language? What is your status?

But there's a way to return to the source of indigeneity without falling into clichés. We don't have to stick feathers in our hair simply for the spectacle of the thing. If the same rituals are performed over and over the same way, they lose some of their force. We have to bring them into the present. If I turn to my Indigenous values to find creative inspiration, I can come up with new rituals. But in order to do that, I have to reject some of our old traditions, such as the idea of serving men first. The land—including the humans, animals, plants, and minerals on it—remains the primary source of knowledge for Indigenous people. The name of this place where we are right now, Domain Notcimik, it means "the place where my blood comes from," the woods, the forest. And that's why I asked you to come here to La Tuque from Montreal. That's why I invited you to come here to Atikamekw territory. Because I've come to realize—after a lot of writing—that it was here, on this land, that I developed my own creative process. This is where I feel most comfortable creating.

Life in the forest requires knowledge that is passed down through traditional methods. But we have to pick and choose, we have to experiment, we have to take risks. Like thought itself, ideology is a living thing. It changes.

But traditionally, the religion that was rejected by the anarchists was extremely institutionalized. There was a clergy, a strict hierarchy with the pope at the head, followed by the cardinals, the bishops, and the priests, etc. Some anarchists are against faith itself, on the grounds that God does not exist, and that faith is therefore an illusion or a lie. These anarchists can be harsh with believers of any religion. But others are simply against the institution of religion and the associated religious hierarchies. Spirituality exists in your narrative, but without priests, without spiritual leaders.

Even anarchists have faith. They place their faith in their own ideology: anarchism. It's a powerful emotional connection. I think that everyone has direct contact with a kind of spirituality, whether they are prepared to admit it or not. If you are against religion or spirituality in such a forceful, aggressive way, it simply means that there is room within you to reflect on these types of questions. If you are aware that you have a spirit that might have an effect on your being, you have a connection with your spirituality, which is, as I understand it, a connection with the environment, because every living thing has a body and a spirit. Catholicism has simply understood this concept in a way that is more abstract, with more references to evil and hell, in order to maintain moral control over believers.

Were you ever a Catholic?

I was baptized, but I haven't been to mass since I was 16 years old. Back then, I went to mass with my grandparents, because they were part of the Indigenous community made up of practicing Catholics, as are many Indigenous people in Latin America. But there was a parting of ways. My grandparents were very Catholic, but I chose not to practice Catholicism so that I could rediscover the Indigenous spiritual traditions. These traditions were passed on through culture, often from our elders. And they have changed over time. But that's a whole other issue.

I want to address the question of racial mixing. Sometimes you introduce yourself as Atikamekw, other times as Métis.

It's one of the great dualities of my life! When you live in an Indigenous community and your father is white you're considered to be a little white girl. A Métisse. But when you live outside of an Indigenous community and your mother is Indigenous, you're automatically Indigenous, a little Indian. I grew up with these two realities, straddled between these two cultures. I was never able to say where I came from, only that I came from the area between Mauricie and the Laurentians. And when I started to write plays, I said, "I'm not just Atikamekw, I'm Quebecois as well." There's a large part of my identity that I never used to acknowledge, but in the end, I'm not only Atikamekw, I'm also Métis. And that is a gift to me. But I introduce myself as Atikamekw instead of Métis, so as not to be mistaken for Plains Métis. And what does métis even mean, anyway? It means mixed race, so there can be métis who are mixed Quebecois and African, or mixed Atikamekw and African, etc. "Métis" is an overarching, generalized term. It would be more accurate to call me an Atikamekw Métisse.

Many white Quebecois have discovered that they had an Indige-nous ancestor in their family tree and subsequently started calling themselves Métis, even if they have no ties whatsoever to Indig-

enous lands or communities. And in Quebec, there's the issue of cultural appropriation, for example in the film L'empreinte. Some individuals who have no direct relationships with Indigenous communities even call themselves Métis to support arguments that oppose the Indigenous cause.

I think that if you're interested in Indigenous people, you should start by listening to them and supporting their stories, and by accepting their political and territorial claims. The governments of Quebec and Canada have a lot of difficulty recognizing Indigenous rights, but the general population likes to appropriate elements of Indigenous culture. Just look at all the cars with dream catchers hanging from the rearview, all the clothes decorated with Indigenous patterns. And there's a big difference between the actions of the government and those of the population. People might be interested in First Nations culture, and they might end up appropriating that culture, like in the example of those infamous rearview dream catchers. But that's to be expected in this globalized world. Even among us Atikamekw, we have appropriated certain symbols that were never part of our traditions or ancestral practices. And we're borrowing objects and customs from around the world. Trucks, TVs: these things aren't Atikamekw in origin, but we use them. And that's normal, because human beings are always trying to build connections with others. Cultures are shared, cultures change. No culture in the world remains identical over time. However, maybe Quebecois people who discover that they have Indigenous roots should support First Nations peoples in their struggle to force the government to recognize their rights. That would be the bare minimum of what should happen.

Theater allows me to create new ideals and new references, to rethink Indigenous ways of expressing myself and taking action. It lets me take that step back from the world of art and politics, especially in view of the Indigenous art industry and the Indigenous political sphere. There's a lot of demand for Indigenous content, especially in the context of Montreal's 375th anniversary, but really, that celebration has nothing to do with us. Both the Indigenous artists protesting the anniversary and those who are organizing it and participating in it are exploiting the zeitgeist, to a certain extent. You can denounce the situation and make it into a key talking point for your protest movement, but at the same time, it's 2017 and Indigenous artists are being invited to participate in the present context of reconciliation. It's difficult for Indigenous artists living in the city, or anywhere else for that matter, to avoid being politicized, particularly with all the budget cuts in the arts, despite the governments' promises. I think that bringing an anarcho-indigenist perspective to aboriginal cultural production would demonstrate that some freedoms are too often accessible only to those who have significant financial and organizational means.

Freda Huson and Toghestiy

Interviewed by Amani Khalfan
First published in *Upping the Anti*, no. 17, 2015.
Thanks to the editors for the authorization to republish this interview.

Unist'ot'en Camp (British Columbia) — environmental-
ism and traditionalism — struggles against pipelines and the
oil industry — defending life and the territory — the band
council system

When Canada's fossil fuel industry launched an aggressive plan to turn the country into a major energy exporter
and triple tar sands production by 2030, few of its supporters could have foreseen the Indigenous-led resistance
that has now delayed or blocked almost every proposed
mega-pipeline. Grassroots organizing in British Columbia
has thus far frustrated efforts by industry and government
to build pipelines to the Pacific coast. These pipelines, by
facilitating export of the dirtiest fuels on the planet to international markets, would allow Canada to massively expand
its tar sands and LNG (liquefied natural gas) industries.

The Unist'ot'en Camp, situated in Northwest BC, stands
out as an uncompromising site of resistance to pipelines and to colonization. It is a community determined
to protect sovereign Wet'suwet'en territory from several
proposed tar sands and fracked gas pipelines. Established
in 2009, the camp is one of the continent's longest-running
active blockades. Supporters have built cabins, pithouses,
and permaculture gardens directly on the GPS coordinates

104

of several proposed pipelines. They enforce a Consent Protocol that determines who is allowed access to the area, and have evicted pipeline crews found working on Wet'su-wet'en territory several times. Pipelines being blockaded include Enbridge's Northern Gateway,[1] Chevron's Pacific Trails,[2] and TransCanada's Coastal GasLink[3] and Prince Rupert projects.[4]

Freda Huson and Toghestiy, Wet'suwet'en land defenders and representatives of the camp, live permanently on the blockade. Freda (Unist'ot'en Clan) is spokesperson of the camp, and Toghestiy is a hereditary chief of the Likhts'amisyu Clan. Amani Khalfan interviewed them in October 2014.

Could you put the Unist'ot'en struggle against pipelines in context? What sort of industry has impacted your territories most? Who and what has been affected?

Toghestiy: I wrote a report for the Unist'ot'en about five years ago explaining the cumulative impact of industry on our territories. It started way back when the Unist'ot'en as well as the other Wet'suwet'en were forcibly removed from the territories and put onto Indian reserves. There was a forced disconnection from the land that was really tough because a lot of family members didn't make it. They either froze or starved to death. We weren't allowed off those reserves, so we had to find ways to survive there. Before contact, our people thrived and had a lot of food and health benefits from being out on our traditional lands. Reserves were the first big impact and they blazed the way for industry to make its way into the

---

1   This project was abandoned in 2016.

2   This project is still under review and one of its parts (Kitimat LNG) bene-fited from an agreement with the Haisla nation.

3   This project is still under review and is supposed to reach Kitimat.

4   Still under review.

territories. Not long thereafter, small logging camps started to open up, and the railroad came in.

Eventually in 1952 there was a hydroelectric project slated for Kitimat, called the Kemano Project. There's a huge man-made lake that spans the southern part of the Wet'suwet'en territories called Ootsa Lake. The company dammed the entire area and flooded a massive span of land that belonged to the Unist'ot'en. They drilled a massive tunnel through a mountain, and the water in the reservoir flowed through the tunnel to turn giant turbines, which generated electricity for the Alcan aluminum smelter. Through that process, the Wet'suwet'en nation lost a massive caribou herd that used to migrate down into Secwepemc country near Kamloops and north through Wet'suwet'en territory up into Gitxsan territory. All the caribou drowned when they were trying to cross over the reservoir following their migratory routes. Up until 1952, caribou was our staple food.

After that, mining, agricultural, and logging companies began to create a huge footprint on the land. Settlers migrated in by the hundreds, establishing homesteads that were initially cleared by Wet'suwet'en people; they basically kicked Wet'suwet'en families out of their homes, killed their cattle, burned their buildings down, and took over the land.

More recently the small logging and mining companies have begun to amalgamate and create bigger projects. Now we have one really big logging company in Wet'suwet'en territories, the Canfor forest company. Our people have been impacted by mining companies destroying watersheds. One of the big ones was the Equity Silver Mine disaster in 1984 when a tailings pond burst and wiped out a huge salmon run that used to make its way up close to Freda's dad's territory.

We've also faced a lot of agricultural expansion. Grazing leases were handed out to farmers to bring their cattle out, and eventually these farmers fenced off a large area of the bush and converted that into private land. The Ministry of Forests and the Ministry of Environment handed over this land to the farmers because they invested so much time and energy into it. Because of that, quite a few people are landowners of Wet'suwet'en territory. There was no consultation with the people at all. Even today, the Ministry of Forests is facilitating landowners in taking massive swaths of unceded Wet'suwet'en land. Even if we challenge them, they continue to hand out permits.

More recently we're dealing with pipeline companies. Fracking pipelines and bitumen pipelines are being proposed to bulldoze their way right through our territories. Our people are all facing up to them. And that's where Freda and her clan stepped up.

You have said that people always ask you how you became activists or environmentalists, but that you're not—you're traditionalists. What is traditionalism and how does this approach influence your strategies and actions?

Freda: We grew up this way, as traditionalists, learning how to only take what you need and how to always give back—industry doesn't do that. Logging companies have clear-cut massive sections and actually tripled their allowable cut. They use these machines that just tear up the ground. They say, "Well, logging is a renewable resource because we plant trees back." But they only put back the species that they plan to cut down again, like balsam, spruce, and pine.

It's quite dry and the soil is dead everywhere they've clear-cut. The same vegetation doesn't grow back. The whole ecosystem is out of balance because of it. It impacts all the animals; we've noticed there are fewer and fewer of certain species and when some of the forests are allowed to grow back, you see these species start resurfacing again. Then the company comes along and does more clear-cutting.

Our people have always used all our territories according to the seasons. For our salmon, we went back to the home community where we grew up to do our fishing. Certain areas are more plentiful with moose, so we usually ran our hunting camps in one of our other territories. And this area that we're protecting from the pipelines is one of the best for trapping. Each of our territories had a specific purpose, and we still practice that today.

Our berry picking has been impacted because clear-cutting wipes out our medicines and berry patches. As Toghestiy mentioned, farmers and ranchers branch out on to territories where we normally hunt. They've put up fences that say "no trespassing" and they have cattle guards everywhere so the moose can't roam freely anymore. They've clear-cut a lot of the areas and now there's grass there. So more and more, it's looking like farmland when it's supposed to be forest. That causes an imbalance for the atmosphere too, and the lake is not the same. We should be able to drink out of the lake but now we can't because the cattle have polluted it.

At what point did you decide that it was necessary to start living on the blockade, in the path of the pipelines?

Freda: It was probably five years ago when we started talking about our concerns and saying we had to do something. We put up the cabin, but nobody was actually living here and we were finding we couldn't effectively monitor our territory. My dad always said that the strongest thing that you can do is to actually occupy, to show that you're still using that land—and then they won't be able to remove you because it's not just a blockade. We're actually living here, and we're occupying our land and reclaiming our responsibility.

Even now we're practicing conservation; we're not allowing hunters in. We're trying to let the population replenish, then once there are a lot more moose we can open up again—maybe to our people and not to the general public, because our people are having a hard time finding moose. Everybody else's staple food is beef and chicken; our staple food is fish, moose, deer, and everything we get off the land.

Toghestiy: Another thing we noticed over the past few months is a herd of caribou that were reintroduced to Wet'suwet'en territory. They were transplanted in the mountain range north of us as an experiment, and they're doing well now. We actually sighted some caribou in the back of the territory behind the blockade. It's the first time we've seen caribou in this part of Wet'suwet'en territory since before 1952. We know that if we let the hunters in somebody might accidentally shoot one of them and we don't want that to happen, so we decided to close it off this year.

There was a hunter who came in who was really irate, and threatened to kill us. That's what we're dealing with now. And it's bizarre. Why are they so insistent that they have to come in here? A lot of these hunters think it's like the African Serengeti back here because there's a bloackade, but in fact there are hardly any moose here; there are some bear and caribou and elk that just started to establish themeselves. We want this place to be available for Unist'ot'en children that are going to grow up. We want them to be able to do what we're doing.

Like Freda said, we're not environmentalists, we're traditionalists. We're managing the lands properly, like they should've been managed all along.

What you're doing here has inspired a lot of people across Turtle Island and further away to become supporters. What do you think motivates and inspires such a wide cross-section of people to support the camp? Do you think more people are coming to understand the importance of grassroots actions ?

Toghestiy: I've heard a lot of people say, "In what other area can you commit all of your energy and actually see physical results being produced, manifesting before your eyes, just through your energy and your input and your belief that it's going to happen?"

People want to see change in human behavior toward how resources on this Earth are managed. A lot of people really think that this place is going to represent that change. You look at the oil companies, the logging companies, the mining companies—they're completely destroying what's left of our environment.

We're in crisis mode, but we're not behaving like it because the general population is distracted from what's really going on by mainstream media, by pop culture, by movies, music, and Facebook. Most people never put their foot down on a peiece of land that is old growth because everything has been developed, and most people lock themselves into a lifestyle that disconnects them from reality.

Freda: I strongly believe that we're doing what we're doing so that we're prepared when everything collapses. The planet cannot keep going the way it's going. Pretty soon all the agriculturalists aren't going to be able to grow food like they once were; the way they're mass-producing, they're destroying the soil. It takes a long time for soil to replenish itself. Oil and gas will not be here forever, and the whole planet is dependent on that industry to manufacture all that processed food everybody eats. If the weather doesn't cooperate and the land has been impacted so much that all the vegetation dies, what will the animals eat?

Toghestiy: There are a lot of prophecies around the world, especially on Turtle Island, about this. The Wet'suwet'en have a prophecy about what's to come. We have one significant glacier that sits right in the middle of our territories, and the prophecy says that when that glacier melts away, the Earth will catch on fire. Our people need to be prepared if we're to survive. That's always in the back of our minds. We're always thinking, how are we going to prepare for surviving in really rough conditions? How do we put seed away? How do we put food away? How do we store water? Where are some places of refuge?

That's exactly what we're doing here; we're preparing. Our ancestors survived the Great Depression; we had no idea that the Great Depression was even here until the settlers started showing up at our doorsteps. Our people who survived the first couple of decades on Indian reserves began to thrive again because we were survivors.

Freda: More and more people are talking about doing the very thing we're doing, because they're realizing that it is actually working. When we stayed confined in the prison of the reserves, industry was continuing business as usual. Since we reoccupied, people have to ask our permission to come onto the territory. But people still freely come and go on our other territories because we can only fight one battle at a time.

On the bridge over the [Wedzin Kwah] River that leads to this territory we have a sign that says "No access without consent." We don't give people permission to come in unless they answer a series of questions: who they are; why they are here; how long they plan to stay; whether they work for industry or government that's destroying our lands; and how their visit will benefit our people. That last one is key. If it won't benefit our people and if it will negatively impact our lands, we're not going to permit entry.

We were hoping that once we showed people we could do this successfully, others would join us. Right now we have a neighbor 40 minutes drive from us who has moved into a cabin and is doing what we're doing. They're trying to protect their territory from a tailings pond and mine that's proposed for the lake next to their cabin.

Toghestiy: We're not just fighting the pipeline; we're fighting colonization. Colonization is rearing its ugly head because colonization is basically the industrialization of this planet. Governments are in place to facilitate the voracious industrial appetite for resources that don't belong to them in the first place.

We have the Delgamuukw court case, and now we have the Tsilhqot'in case.[5] Our people are bolstered by this. But you know, that's not the only reason why we're here. Our traditional laws dictate that our people should be doing exactly what we're doing. And it's not just our people; it's all Indigenous people. I think a lot of First Nations people are getting that: they're realizing that if they stay in their Indian reserves or urban centers and just exist in the system, nothing's going to change. But if they get onto their ancestral lands, they'll see exactly what's happening to them and begin answering the call of their ancestors to protect them. That's really inspiring for us.

What sort of tactics have the provincial and federal governments used in attempting to delegitimize your resistance or dissolve your resolve? How have they approached you or tried to deal with the Unist'ot'en Camp?

Freda: They haven't. They're saying that the only legitimate organization or legal entity they choose to recognize is the band council. To me, band councils have never had jurisdiction off the reserves and they don't have any decision-making

---

5   In the *Delgamuukw v. British Columbia* case, the Supreme Court of Canada acknowledged that an Indigenous title is still an ancestral right protected by the 1982 Constitution. This brought the recognition that oral history is valid proof of ancestral title. The Tsilhqot'in nation then used this case in their own struggles for title recognition, the Supreme Court has acknowledged their title since then.

powers because the federal government makes all the policies that govern how the Indian Act Bands operate. But the federal government is trying to say they're the only people they recognize because they decide for the reserves. They're using that as an excuse to push forward even though bands don't have jurisdiction off the reserves. We proved it through Delgamuukw, through their highest Supreme Court: the hereditary chiefs[6] and their members have a legitimate claim to the Wet'suwet'en territory.

What the government and these companies have done is extract resources from our territories and then give crumbs to the bands to operate on. They've deliberately impoverished our peoples so that they can dangle a carrot in front of them. A lot of our people are struggling, and the leadership is thinking they're doing good by trying to sign these deals—even though they're for crumbs compared to the billions of dollars from a pipeline project. When the government decided they wanted these pipeline projects to go through, they said there was an "Indian problem" they needed to get rid of. Brian Mulroney and a bunch of other ex-prime ministers sat down and dreamed up this idea of putting money forward from the federal government to start what they called the First Nations Limited Partnership to try and get the bands to sign on to

---

6   The Canadian reservation system creates a difference between the elected leaders who have a seat on band councils (the official Indigenous governmental structure imposed by the Canadian state through the Indian Act) and the hereditary or traditional chiefs, whose influence is more informal. Traditional chiefs' legitimacy mainly stems from their protection and use of ancestral customs and territories, which often puts them at odds with the band council system. This being said, it sometimes happens that people switch titles, depending on the power (im)balances in each community. For instance, while Toghestiy was hereditary chief of the Likhts'amisyu Clan when he was interviewed in 2014, he has since become chief on his band council. See also his own criticism towards corruption among traditional chiefs in the last part of this interview.

Chevron's Pacific Trails Pipeline, so that they could say they have Indigenous support.[7]

The 2014 Supreme Court decision recognized the Tsilhqot'in nation's title to a large area of traditional territory in BC sets a precedent for Indigenous land rights. What needs to be done to establish those rights on the ground?

Toghestiy: Our people need to begin doing exactly what we're doing. Our people need to begin moving out onto their territories, managing them the way their ancestors did. They need to design a protocol process that determines who they let into or prohibit from their territories. If we don't do that, all will be lost forever. Nobody else will do it for our people.

Unfortunately, a lot of our people are in survival mode right now. We're living life day-to-day, making sure that we can still find enough money to pay the rent, to put food on the table. As Freda explained, our people are put into a poverty situation and we're still in survival mode. A large part of our diet, because we live in poverty, is processed foods, and that's killing our people with diabetes, and with obesity. We need to be learning how to live off of our lands, learning how to harvest animals and plants and medicines the way our ancestors did so that we can begin to live healthy again.

Is that part of the reason you argue that instead of thinking about human "rights," we need to start thinking about "responsibilities"?

Toghestiy: Absolutely. Rights contain the assumption that somebody has given you the ability to act out your respon-

---

7   This state tactics seems to have had some success; Chevron now boasts of their so-called agreements with 16 First Nations whose territories are on the path of the Pacific Trail project. See https://canada.chevron.com/our-businesses/kitimat-lng-project/pacific-trail-pipeline.

sibility. Rights create the illusion that somebody somewhere is going to say, "Okay. I'm going to give you this permission, my permission—and I hope you feel special about it—to act out your responsibilities." That's where the mistake lies, at the beginning of that thought process.

In order for us to exist as human beings on this planet, we have to take a really good look at our responsibilities as human beings. Rights are only there because we have this idea that somebody somewhere is going to give us those rights. That's not how it works. We have a responsibility to treat each other well, to treat each other with respect.

If we start looking at responsibilities, maybe things will change. That's what we did here with our permaculture garden. We went into a place that was clear-cut, where the soil was dead. It was our responsibility to the land to find a way to nurture that soil back to life. Now we have a vibrant permaculture garden, but that took a lot of work.

Everybody should stop thinking about trying to be a good citizen of the country that imposes itself on them and instead focus on becoming a good citizen of the planet. All of our ancestors were like that at one time.

What do you think that would mean for international solidarity with people with similar struggles for sovereignty, in places where there's a higher level of impunity for government and industry who use force to get communities out of the way of development?

Toghestiy: We have the responsibility to make sure that those people are supported. Not just morally, but by getting out there and actually doing something tangible. A lot of people visit our website or the Victoria Forest Action Network website and find a way to support us.[8] A lot of people come out and

---

8   See www.fankenya.org.

do stuff voluntarily for us: they spend a week, a month, a year. They want to contribute what they can because they know it's making a difference. It's a tangible difference, not an abstract idea.

When grassroots people want to get out and start looking after the land because they want to live up to the responsibilities their ancestors had, they should be supported in a real way. We need to set up an international network of people who are inspired to go and do something like that. We need to make sure that they're protected, and that their children are protected, so that they can nurture that part of their soul that understands what responsibilities are, and live up to those responsibilities in a really good way.

People in Ecuador have also been fighting Chevron for decades. What are the links between their struggle and yours?

Toghestiy: Our sisters and brothers in Ecuador are suffering from the industrial decisions Chevron made in their backyards. Chevron had pipelines running through the Ecuadorian rainforest and oil wells that weren't containing the oil properly. The government and corporations were corrupt and were hiding these spills. And then people started dying. The Ecuadorian court ruled that Chevron had to pay for the spills, and Chevron packed up and moved out.

Recently the Canadian Bar Association was attempting to intervene on behalf of Chevron, in the Supreme Court of Canada case where Chevron will be challenged for what they did in Ecuador. There was a huge uproar in Toronto, and the Bar Association decided to back down because of the public pressure. That's what needs to happen here.

We're fully aware that Chevron is trying to get a pipeline through our territories. They came right into our communities, we saw them and asked them questions. It was ludicrous, listening to them. I said point blank, "You guys are responsible for what happened in Ecuador. Now you're trying to come into our backyards and do the same old thing and you expect us to ignore your history." They tried to explain their way out of it and they couldn't. The community just sat there and watched these guys fumble their words.

We have decided to join forces with people in Ecuador who are fighting Chevron. Over the next year we're going to be doing a lot of things in conjunction to bolster our fight against Chevron, because they're attempting to set up shop in other countries and totally dismiss the fact that the countries where they did the damage are trying to hold them accountable. What they've done is atrocious. They should be held responsible.

Given that history, can you describe how Chevron and other companies are working to get support in your community, to get people to believe that they are capable of being the good neighbors they advertise themselves as?

Toghestiy: The corporations Chevron and Apache are working on the Pacific Trails Pipeline in our territory. They've actually taken quite a few people from our home community of Moricetown[9]—community members, band councillors, and their families—and flown them out on a private jet to Calgary and Vancouver and to Fort St. John where the fracking fields are. They've entertained them in these places, given them massive honoraria, and convinced them that natural gas is safe. Industry and government are spending millions of dollars every year to fool the general public that fracked gas is the same as natural gas, when it's very different.

---

9   Wet'suwet'en village (British Columbia, Canada).

In the more recent development, in June or July 2014, the Moricetown band was attempting to sign a deal with Chevron and Apache for the Pacific Trails Pipeline. The first draft of that deal was leaked and we got access to it. If they'd signed it, this is what they would have gotten away with: after five years of running the pipeline, Chevron and Apache would be able to sell it to a bitumen company—a tar sands company, like Enbridge and Kinder Morgan, like all these other fools who want to run this mock oil into international markets.

As soon as we saw that, our suspicions were confirmed. Now they say, "Well, the new deal we're doing with the band says we can never ever sell it as bitumen." But what they leave out of that statement is "Unless the First Nations Limited Partnership agrees that it's okay to do so." The people in the First Nations Limited Partnership are very corrupt leaders of Indian bands. If they decide they want to make a lot of money selling a fracking pipeline to a bitumen company, that's what they'll do. If they become members of this First Nations Limited Partnership group, they'll have decision-making powers that don't require them to consult with their own community members.

Do you think there's a possibility that Moricetown band will sign this agreement with Chevron and Apache?[10]

Toghestiy: We almost got them the last time we had a meeting in Moricetown. The community was just outraged that the band council was even considering it. The chief councillor was going to get up and say that Moricetown band will

---

10   In January 2015, the Moricetown band council joined the First Nations Limited Partnership created by Chevron. See www.newswire.ca/news-releases/moricetown-indian-band-joins-first-nations-limited-partnership-516510191.html; and https://news.gov.bc.ca/stories/moricetown-band-partners-on-lng-pipeline-agreements.

not consider signing a deal with that company, but one of the hereditary chiefs stopped him and said, "no, sit down, don't say that." And they decided to see if they could negotiate another deal with that company. It's bizarre: one of our hereditary chiefs stopped the elected chief from saying that they will not be signing any deals with pipeline companies. So, the corruption isn't just among the elected chiefs, it's beginning to be spread among the hereditary chiefs who are willing to get wined and dined by these guys. This one hereditary chief that stopped the elected chief gets hockey tickets to go watch the Canucks play in Vancouver. He gets season tickets in one of those private boxes. That's his motivation to keep these pipeline companies really close. I'm not afraid to say that because it's the truth.

A lot of the struggles that we're facing today are people not living up to their responsibilities—not just the chiefs, but the house members themselves. We need to find hereditary chiefs who understand that the territories need to be protected for future generations. Hereditary chiefs have a responsibility to look after the territories and determine when too many resources have been taken. That's not happening. A lot of our hereditary chiefs today don't even spend time out on their traditional territories. I don't like saying that in public, especially in a public interview, but it's the truth. It pains me to see our people struggling because we've allowed some hereditary chiefs to come into power who aren't connected to the lands, who aren't making sure that the future generations will benefit from the decisions they make today. Hereditary chiefs are supposed to be very selfless in their decision-making.

There is already a lot of opposition to the Énergie Est tar sands pipeline that TransCanada plans to build from Alberta through Quebec, Ontario, and New Brunswick. Based on how your struggle has evolved, what guidance can you share for people resisting that pipeline?

Toghestiy: People need to realize that they're not going to have the full support of their community right off the bat. That will grow over time. They need to have faith in the decisions that they're going to be making to begin exercising the responsibilities that they have as grassroots members of their communities who want to see a better future for their people. If people are going to succeed at stopping the pipeline project, they're going to have to come out and just do it. They can't sit back and hope that their cousins or their best friends are going to finally step up and do something. They're going to have to get out and do it themselves.

What do you think are the responsibilities of non-Indigenous allies in terms of support or solidarity work with Indigenous resistance?

Freda: I think it's everybody's responsibility to wake up and realize that if everything continues as it is, and if they continue to destroy the water via fracking, tar sands, mining, and even this foolish proposed pipeline, there won't be any more fresh drinking water. And if you kill off the water, everything else goes with it. Vegetation won't be possible; animals will be contaminated.

People need to go back to the basics, where—not only Indigenous people, I'm pretty sure wherever people came from—they took care of the water, and just took enough to sustain themselves and their families. It's your responsibility to change the mentality that you have to have more of everything in order to feel like you're alive. If you destroy this planet, you destroy yourself.

Toghestiy: This is going to be our sixth year of resistance against pipeline companies, but we've been resisting industry for a long time. That's something our people should be doing all the time—not just Indigenous people but settlers as well. We need to protect the waters and set in motion a trajectory that will allow waters to be decontaminated, to reclaim areas, to work hard to allow them to return to their original state. Right now, things are going in the opposite direction: aquifers and watersheds are being destroyed because of industry and because of what government is allowing them to do.

I think all settlers need to become real, strong, tangible allies with the Indigenous resistance. There are a lot of Indigenous people who are suffering in their homelands right now because industry and government are destroying everything that they need to maintain their cultural identity. If people are aware of that and are actually sympathetic toward that, they need to really think about decolonizing. They need to decolonize their thinking and their decision-making, decolonize the way that they participate in society, and begin working with Indigenous people who need that help.

Update

In January 2015, the Moricetown band council voted in favor of two agreements related to pipeline construction work: TransCanada's Coastal GasLink project and Chevron's Pacific Trails project (through the First Nations Limited Partnership). Meanwhile, the Unist'ot'en Camp kept on growing, particularly through the installation of new traplines in Wet'suwet'en territory and the erection of a health center for Native youth on site.

In May 2015, the Unist'ot'en Camp sent out a call to urgent action while TransCanada started prospecting Wet'suwet'en territory to initiate the Coastal GasLink project. Chevron was also given a green light by the BC Oil and Gas Commission for clearing a passage to build the Pacific Trails Pipeline.

In January 2019, the BC Supreme Court filed an injunction against the Unist'ot'en Camp even though a judicial process (initiated in the fall of 2018 by the National Energy Board (NEB)) looking at possible legal violations by the TransCanada project was underway. On January 7, armed with this injunction, the RCMP launched a large and aggressive paramilitary operation against the camp to take down the Wet'suwet'en blockade. All media were barred from accessing the site and surrounding areas by the police force, which also set up signal jamming and communication disruption devices to prevent media coverage of ongoing operations, essentially repeating the methods used during the RCMP attack on Ts'Peten / Gustafsen Lake in 1995. Fourteen land defenders were arrested that day (charges against them would be dropped in April 2019). The RCMP then occupied Gidimt'en (one of the five clans of the Wet'suwet'en nation) territory in violation of Wet'suwet'en sovereignty as recognized by Canadian law (*Delgamuukw v. British Columbia*, 1997), with the intention of establishing a police detachment on Gidimt'en territory.

Construction work started soon after and on January 26, Coastal GasLink workers willfully, illegitimately, and violently destroyed Gidimt'en cultural infrastructure, personal property and traplines, in direct violation of both Canadian law and agreements between TransCanada and the Wet'suwet'en. While present on site and watching events unfold, with all legal powers to prevent such breach of law, and assisted by liaison officers specialized in intercultural mediation, the RCMP refused to intervene even after receiving multiple formal and judicial complaints by members of the Wet'suwet'en nation who filed criminal charges of destruction of property and mischief against Coastal GasLink. However, instead of issuing a cease and desist order against CGL for the destruction of archeological and cultural heritage sites as requested by the Wet'suwet'en Hereditary Chiefs, Justice Church decided on December 31, 2019, to grant CGL a permanent injunction against Wet'suwet'en land defenders.

In January 2020, two new camps were established along the planned pipeline trail by land defenders, leading to another heavily militarized RCMP operation on February 7 and 8 during which 14 land defenders were arrested. Fourteen other people would be arrested in the following days.

On November 18, 2021, the RCMP conducted another heavily militarized operation against land defenders blockading two of CGL's work camps, arresting 14 people. The next day, the RCMP raided another location of cultural importance to the Wet'suwet'en, known as Wedzin Kwa, where land defenders had set up camp in September. Among people arrested that day were two journalists; charges against them would be dropped, in contrast to the four additional people they were with.

In July 2022, on the advice of Justice Church, the Crown decided to further criminalize Wet'suwet'en land defenders by pressing criminal charges against four of the people arrested by the RCMP in November, bringing the total number of people facing criminal contempt charges for opposing CGL to 19.

In the words of Wet'suwet'en Hereditary Chief Na'Moks, "It's really reconciliation at the end of a gun."

J. Kēhaulani Kauanui

Discovering American anarchism — Hawai'i — the Occupy movement — the United States context — the Māori — Palestine — feminism and queerness — how to talk about anarchism at the university and on the radio

J. Kēhaulani Kauanui is a diasporic Kanaka Maoli (Native Hawaiian) born in southern California on the traditional homeland of the Tongva people, and raised there as well as in Acjachemen territory further south. She currently lives in Mattabessett (known as Middletown, Connecticut), where she lives and works on the historic lands of the Wangunk people as a professor of American Studies and affiliate in Anthropology at Wesleyan University. There she teaches courses related to Indigenous studies, critical race studies, settler colonial studies, and anarchist studies. Her books include *Hawaiian Blood: Colonialism and the Politics of Sovereignty and Indigeneity* (2008) and *Paradoxes of Hawaiian Sovereignty: Land, Sex, and the Colonial Politics of State Nationalism* (2008). Kauanui is also the editor of *Speaking of Indigenous Politics: Conversations with Activists, Scholars, and Tribal Leaders* (2018), which features select interviews from her radio program, "Indigenous Politics: From Native New England and Beyond," which she produced and hosted solo for seven years. Kauanui currently serves as a co-producer for an anarchist politics show called, "Anarchy on Air," a majority people-of-color show co-produced with a group of students.

What is your understanding of "anarcho-indigenism"?

124

I have thought about that question, in general, quite a lot. For me, it is a commitment to Indigenous self-determination with an anarchist orientation—actively opposing colonial domination—a broad political practice critical of statist nationalism, unjustified authority, and domination in all forms.

What was your first encounter with anarchism, or anarchists?

I can identify several events that transpired over the course of a two-year period that stand out—those episodes in my own trajectory shaped my attraction to anarchist sensibilities. The first was when I traveled to San Francisco right after graduating from high school in 1986. It was my first vacation as an adult and I went with my best friend, Amberlyn. We paid for the trip ourselves and because we were on a limited budget, we stayed at the YWCA for a good part of it. One of our first stops was the Height-Ashbury district of the city—a site of 1960s counterculture that had loomed large for us as 1980s kids. There we found Bound Together Anarchist Collective Bookstore, which is still up and running. I combed every inch of that store, but especially gravitated to the many political pamphlets.

Another formative moment was the next year, in 1987, when I was based at Cambridge University for a summer study abroad program (offered through the community college in Irvine, California, where I was enrolled at the time). I went to every festival and leftist protest I could find—my escape from behind "the Orange Curtain" (as many of us referred to Orange County), since it was during Ronald Reagan's presidency and he was especially revered in the area where I had been living. Anyhow, at one of the gatherings I went to, there were anarchists' tables with fliers and pamphlets. I picked up all I could, read anything and everything I could get my hands on, and just sat with it. At the time, though, I was still committed to the Democratic Party, which was close to heresy in southern California, given how neoconservative the political climate was. I was just 19.

The following year, while I was doing outreach for voter registration (as one of my many paid jobs), I remember stumping for Michael Dukakis. I had been a supporter of Jessie Jackson, but when Dukakis won the democratic primary, I got behind him. At the time, I was willing to support just about anyone who ran against George H. W. Bush. Anyhow, I recall this one night, after pounding the pavement in Santa Ana going door-to-door asking people to register to vote and encouraging them to support the ticket. I was working along-side my friend Tim, and when we were done for the evening we went to our mutual friend Betsy's house. There I finally met her (by then) notorious cousin Piet, the one I had heard about for years—an anarchist punk visiting from Berkeley. He got wind of what Tim and I had been up to that night and immediately started to problematize the Democrats, and electoral politics in general. He spoke very eloquently as I listened intently, whereas Tim got very defensive since he heard this as needling antagonism. I was, on the other hand, very intrigued. Everything he said resonated with me in a deep way; I could not argue with any of his points. I had been carrying around my own questions about liberation for the two years prior—mostly through the work of radical women-of-color feminists—and it felt like a door was opening. The follow-ing year, I traveled back to the Bay Area again, but this time had the chance to visit Piet at the cooperative he lived in, the now defunct—yet, still infamous—Barrington Hall, which was a student housing cooperative affiliated with the University Students' Cooperative Association in Berkeley. I knew the minute I walked in that I wanted to live there and did just that later the same year when I transferred from Irvine Valley College to UC Berkeley.

In the meantime, while still in southern California, I had been involved in reproductive politics and some clinic defense and other direct actions at Planned Parenthood. Through that milieu, I came to learn about DIY women's health care, called "self-help" at the time. I read about the Jane Collective—also known as the Abortion Counseling Service of Women's Liberation. Every fiber in my body said yes. I then got ahold of the book *A New View of a Woman's Body*, put out by the Federation of Feminist Women's Health Center. Besides the many ways the text was body positive (all shapes, sizes, and colors), it laid out the basics of cervical and breast self-exams, radical lessons of the biology of the clitoris, as well as menstrual extraction (a form of vacuum aspiration to empty the uterus of menses, but also used as a form of early abortion). Having been raised Catholic, I had grown up with a lot of body shame and was not yet sexually active—so was absolutely riveted by the idea that I could learn for myself about my own body, and also acquire an empowering skill-set that could be learned in a community with other women. Bush had won the election and it looked likely at the time that he would do all he could to make abortions illegal. Hence, soon after moving to Berkeley in the fall of 1989, I found people involved in the reproductive rights movement to see if anyone else knew about the self-help movement. Eventually, I connected with a group of feminists who also wanted to learn about this, and through our networks with people in Oakland we embarked on a journey together to learn as much as we could about reproductive health and our own (and each other's) bodies.

Some Indigenous scholars and activists will claim that anarchists have a lot to learn from "quasi-anarchist" or anarchistic traditional Indigenous political and cultural systems (prior colonization). However, not all Indigenous communities and nations before colonization were "quasi-anarchist," anti-authoritarian, and egalitarian (one might think of the Maya, for instance). In Hawai'i, there was a kingdom, and in 1893 the US government overthrow the reigning monarch, Queen Lili'uokalani. Although this sovereign state comprised Kanaka Maoli (Hawaiian people) and non-Indigenous subjects, it was a state and even a kingdom. Could it still be a reference for anarchists and anarchism?

I would like to start by flipping the first part of your question. I would not say indigenism is anarchist, but that some forms of anarchism are based on selective aspects of indigenism. There are many epistemological differences between Indigenous forms of self-governance (in all their diversity) and Western sovereignty.

In the Hawaiian context, exploring these differences entails an examination of pre-kingdom Kanaka Maoli history and the nineteenth-century European imperialism that led to the formation of the monarchy. Kamehameha established the kingdom in 1810, after forging protracted battle to unify the islands starting in 1795, decades after foreign encroachment. The Hawaiian Kingdom gained international recognition as an independent state by 1843 when Britain, France, and the United States honored its sovereignty. Even then, we need to look at what kind of state the monarchy was. For example, the kingdom's first constitution, promulgated by Kamehameha III, was more progressive than the United States at the time as it affirmed equality under the law for the chiefs and the common people "under one and the same law."

In any case, there are other points of reference that may relate to anarchist sensibilities in terms of how the Indigenous common people lived on the land—the reverence for the *'āina* (literally that which feeds) is front and center; the mountains, streams, winds, animals, and trees are not inanimate objects— they are living entities with names and some of them are the *kinolau* (embodied manifestation) of deities, while others are *'aumākua* (ancestral). But to be sure, precolonial Hawaiian society was quite stratified along the lines of genealogical rank, a chiefly hierarchy.

Although I remain committed to challenging US authority over Hawai'i—and cite international law as a tactic in doing so—I think what is more inspiring for the question in terms of a point of reflection regarding anarchism is the *ahupua'a* system. Each island, or *mokupuni*, was ruled by a paramount chief (*mō'ī*) and divided into large sections, or *moku-o-loko*. These *moku* were further divided into *'okana* or *kalana*—districts—and each district was comprised of many *ahupua'a* (wedge-shaped sections of land). The *mō'ī* allocated *ahupua'a* (traditional land sections) to lesser chiefs who entrusted the land's administration to their local land stewards, the *konohiki*, who in turn administered land access for *maka'āinana* (the common people) who labored for the chiefs and fulfilled tributary. This system has been misrepresented in the Western historiography as feudal, but that was not the case since there was no compulsory military service involved.

The *ahupua'a* were usually wedge-shaped sections of land that followed natural geographical boundaries, such as ridgelines and rivers, and ran from mountain to sea. An *ahupua'a* usually includes all the materials required for sustenance—from the mountains to the sea, and members of the society shared access. As grassroots activist Andre Perez (Kanaka Maoli) put it in a radio interview I conducted with him for the anarchist radio program, "Horizontal Power Hour," which I used to co-produce and co-host,

> [With] the ahupua'a concept—the land bases were all individually set-up. In Hawaii we have a lot of valleys that run mauka to makai, from the mountains to the sea. In those valleys were the villages and the people who lived, and they had their own decentralized power over their valleys, their

water, their land, their resources, their politics—and collectively they made up the nation. The interesting thing is, even with over 120 years of US occupation, colonization, forced assimilation ... we've never lost the sense of the ahupua'a, understanding land division ... the term is still very much paramount now in terms of local politics, government politics ... The ahupua'a concept was a very efficient way to manage the resources in a way that was very sustainable.[1]

Although the *maka'āinana* worked in relationship to the *konohiki* (who in turn were accountable to the paramount chief of said island), looking at the principles of the reverence for the land offers insight into Hawaiian epistemological frames that can be drawn on today for Indigenous revitalization. One of these tenets is that of *aloha 'āina*, love for the land, which is core to Hawaiian values and premised on ecological and spiritual balance, as well as responsibility. It is also important to note that the *maka'āinana* can and did challenge chiefly authority, and the ties between the common people and the chiefs were premised on cultural ethics of reciprocity. But my main point is that it is this relation to land that is a core difference between Indigenous and Western ontologies; in the Western world, land is proprietorialized as a commodity. The French anarchist philosopher Proudhon asserted, "Property is theft!", while Indigenous peoples have always known this.

That said, perhaps instead of Indigenous people trying to prove that Indigenous ways of life can be of use to anarchists, we can refocus to talk about how Indigenous critique can sharpen anarchist thought. For example, the Occupy Wall Street (OWS) movement was an undeniably powerful movement that highlighted the corrosive power of major

---

1   https://archive.org/details/Episode53MapucheResistanceAndHawaiian Self-determination_229.

banks and multinational corporations that entrench the wealth of the 1 percent at the expense of the other 99 percent. And while many of the on-the-ground practices at various #OWS locales relied on non-binding consensus-based collective decisions that resonate with anarchist principles of self-governance, the rallying call was to "reclaim." From the very start dating back to September 2011, Indigenous individuals pointed out how offensive the articulation of the claims as well as the analysis of the problem and the political project itself is on two levels: to assert people "take back Wall Street" and "occupy" given the actual legacy of colonial occupation of the Lenape people's lands and the fact that Wall Street itself was built on the expropriation of Indigenous territory, as well as slavery (which we know through the African burials near where the first slave auction in the city took place in 1655 at Pearl Street and Wall Street). Educators at the National Museum of the American Indian have referred to the "sale of Manhattan" as America's first "urban myth," since there is no known deed of land transfer or bill of sale. And, as Lenape activist-scholar Joanne Barker delineated on her blog site *Tequila Sovereign* during #OWS, in the mid-1600s, the Dutch built the wall that used to stand erect on the actual street called "Wall St." They did so not only to keep out the English, but also block the Lenape Indians from their own territory.

Kuleana (interdependence in a community) and lāhui *(people-hood) are Indigenous concepts referring to collective autonomy. Would you think they may be potentially used by anarchists in their political discussions?*

Kuleana refers to both responsibility and prerogative, and is the foundation for interdependence in community, which is a prerequisite for any healthy and ethical *lāhui*. I do think these Indigenous concepts can be instructive for anarchists.

To learn and understand one's *kuleana* is about accountability and obligation. And it is also knowing what is not our rightful concern or business, so to speak. The thing is, though, I think the concept of *lāhui* is a sticking point for many anarchists who may bristle over the abidance to any notion of distinct peoplehood, which for Indigenous peoples is about survival *as peoples* given the endurance of colonial domination. My sense is that some, or most, (non-Indigenous) anarchists may wince at this notion since it smacks of nationalism. But I largely attribute that to either a myopic view of anarchism being primarily about class struggle, or because they may not have an informed or nuanced view of colonial formations and their effects. I have encountered anarchists who have knee-jerk reactions to any forms of nationalism because they see it as either always already linked to aspirations for state power, or as a form of separatism, patriotism, xenophobia, or ethnic chauvinism—instead of autonomy. Anarchists who criticize those committed to Indigenous distinctions too often condemn in ways that are deeply complicit with settler colonialism and its genocidal logics.

Anarchism is already critical of statism and of the idea of state sovereignty. What does indigenism add to the anarchist criticism of state power and domination?

For me, living in the United States, state power and domination cannot be analyzed, let alone challenged minus an understanding that it is a settler colonial state. Settler colonialism is built to erase Indigenous peoples, as well as cover its own tracks. Hence, a "one-size fits all" anarchist critique of statism and state violence is inadequate.

The Canadian state as well as the United States imposed a racist logic of blood quantum classification on Indigenous people in order to identify who is or isn't Indigenous. How would this way of thinking be alien to indigenism in general, and the Hawaiian Indigenous traditions in particular?

As I have noted in my book, *Hawaiian Blood*, as a colonial imposition, the blood quantum model of identity is a demeaning alternative to Hawaiian kinship and genealogy, which are inclusive and provide a framework for an expansive, Indigenous model of belonging. Moreover, governmental uses of the blood quantum model aim to alter and displace Indigenous forms of identification in a settler colonial bid to deracinate Kanaka Maoli. Blood quantum is about fractions and reduction (vis-à-vis both whites and Asians—the dominant groups in Hawai'i) while Kanaka Maoli genealogy is expansive yet bound to kinship and relations to land and all living entities.

Kanaka Maoli would not see themselves as "Native Americans," or as "Indigenous people of the United States." Why is it so?

The Hawaiian dis-identification with the category of "Native American" has become especially pronounced in the context of the state driven political project to contain the Hawaiian sovereignty claims under international law and subordinate Kanaka Maoli within US domestic policy on Indian tribes. That said, I resist the normalization of US domination over all other Indigenous peoples subject to authority, especially since many Indigenous peoples claimed by the US government also do not identify as Native Americans or as Indigenous peoples *of* the United States. Here we should remember that Indigenous peoples have distinct polities that predate the US government.

You studied the Māori for more than one year, at least; what is one of the most significant things you learned from this experience?

I was enrolled at master's level in the department of Māori Studies at Auckland University in 1994 through a Fulbright fellowship. It was my commitment to solidarity politics that led me there, in addition to the deep cultural and political ties between the Māori and the Hawaiian peoples. The project I originally pitched for my research there was to look at how diasporic Pacific Islanders from other countries interacted with Māori sovereignty struggles. I then wanted to compare that case study to how diasporic Pacific Islanders in California interacted with tribal nations there seeking federal recognition. This research idea came out of my own solidarity with Indigenous peoples and their sovereignty struggles while I was living in the Bay Area working with other Kanaka Maoli in a group I co-founded in 1993 with Sharon Nāwahine LumHo and Paul Kealoha Blake called the Hawaiian Nation Information Group of Northern California. As we worked to educate people in the region about the land struggles in Hawai'i, we were in active solidarity with the Muwekma Ohlone people whose lands we were working on, and their struggle for federal recognition. The solidarity work is bound by the legacies of land dispossession along with some common cultural and political frameworks. There is a global Indigenous "reality," but each people go through different historical-colonial formations.

As it turned out, my project shifted considerably. While in Aotearoa/New Zealand, the national government was designing a unilateral, universal, and *final* settlement that it intended to impose on the Māori *iwi* (tribes)—a package dubbed the "fiscal envelope"—its answer to settling Treaty of Waitangi grievances, limiting the total amount (inclusive of all *iwi* claims) to one billion dollars. The government kept it secret for at least six months before it admitted to having this plan, and I had learned about it at an activist meeting some Māori students at Auckland University had organized after they had gotten a leak from someone working in the government. This was in June 1994 and the government denied it until December of that same year. Anyhow, at that meeting, a new resistance group formed called Te Kawau Mārō. I was invited by the founders to attend future meetings and for the next eleven months traveled with them extensively around the country as they went to various *iwi*-hosted *hui* (gatherings) to spread the word, offer a critique, solicit input from the elders and tribal leaders on the matter, and gather broad-based opposition. The Crown also held a series of consultation *hui* around the country, which I also was fortunate to attend with members of Te Kawau Mārō. Māori vehemently rejected the proposal, especially since the government in advance of the extent of claims being fully known set the monetary limit. The concept of the fiscal envelope was eventually dropped after the 1996 general election, in no small part due to Māori opposition. I had left by May 1995, and was incredibly inspired.

One of the most significant things I learned from this experience was about culturally specific forms of community mobilization and political resistance to colonial forms of settler (descendant) domination. For example, Te Kawau Mārō members traveled to different tribal territories and alerted people in each area within the context of the traditional *hui*, which is shaped by intricate forms of ritual and social protocols—that guided speech itself—specific to each *marae* (meeting ground). This form of mobilization is distinct from forms of protest I was familiar with from the Bay Area (such as shutting down the Bay Bridge to say "no business as usual") though there were marches and other direct actions, but determined by the people of the territory hosting us at each place.

Like many anarchists, other leftists, and even liberals, you are really concerned by the Israeli occupation of Palestine. As an Indigenous person, do you see this issue from a particular point of view?

135

I have been involved in the Boycott, Divestment, and Sanction (BDS) movement since Operation Cast Lead (2008–2009) when the US Campaign for the Academic and Cultural Boycott (USACBI) was launched. I serve on the advisory board and have worked on academic boycott initiatives within three academic associations I am affiliated with: the American Studies Association, the Native American and Indigenous Studies Association, and the American Anthropological Association.

For me this is about many issues, but I come to Palestine in Indigenous solidarity. I have had the opportunity to travel to Palestine twice. The first time was in January 2012 for a five-scholar delegation (comprised of me, Nikhil Singh, Robin D. G. Kelley, Bill V. Mullen, and Neferti Tadiar), organized by USACBI, which was focused on meeting political activists and scholars. The second time in May 2015 was as a participant in a faculty development seminar sponsored by the Palestinian American Research Center, which was to meet with Palestinian scholars in universities in Jerusalem and the West Bank to share common research interests and facilitate intellectual and academic exchange.

What I have found consistent in my time engaged in BDS solidarity politics is that apologists for or defenders of Israel often charge hypocrisy or inconsistency vis-à-vis the history of the United States—that somehow we should not criticize others for having the "same faults." My favorite is when someone says, *People who live in glass houses shouldn't throw stones* in order to suggest that one cannot criticize Israeli settler colonialism given that the United States was founded on the stolen lands of Indigenous peoples. As I have written elsewhere, the politics of indigeneity and a comparative analysis of settler colonialisms bring much to bear on critical analyses of Israeli exceptionalism as it is bolstered and bankrolled by American exceptionalism—the political ideology of divine right in the myth of manifest destiny—which denies the colonization of Native North America. Indeed, the connections between settler colonialism that enable the existence of the United States and Israel are not merely analogous—they are shaped from many of the same material and symbolic forces. But examining those linkages is not the intention of Zionists; for them the charge of duplicity is an attempt to provide cover for Israel.

In my scholarly and activist work exposing and protesting the US occupation of Hawai'i, I routinely challenge the US government's legal claim, expose the roots of the United States as a settler colonial state, and critically engage the history of US imperialism in Native America and its military occupations and/or colonial subordination in Oceania (Guam and the Northern Mariana Islands, as well as American Samoa) and in the Caribbean (the US Virgin Islands and Puerto Rico). Therefore, I find the charge of hypocrisy laughable, especially given that those who typically evoke it have no real interest in challenging US domination in any of these contexts, let alone in the world at large, through its imperial force as the world's superpower.

I should note upfront that I also understand this beyond the occupation—and to get at that we must look at Zionism. I see the occupation and the apartheid system functioning in the service of a broader Israeli settler colonial project—one that is about land expropriation for Israel's ongoing territorial expansion at the expense of the Indigenous people already there, the Palestinians.

In one of her texts, J. Noelani Goodyear-Ka'ōpua argues that the goal of the Hawai'i sovereignty movement should be "how to enact independence rather than call for it." In the same spirit, Glen Coulthard (Yellowknives Dene First Nation) explains that "claims for recognition" are not part of decolonization, since it would necessarily take place within the official structures and institutions of colonialism. What do you make out of this form of recognition by the state?

I agree with both of the scholars you cite—they are brilliant and provocative Indigenous intellectuals whose critical work is some of the best in the field. They speak to the limits and contradictions of recognition—and emphasis Indigenous agency vis-à-vis settler colonial structures and domination. Goodyear-Kaʻōpua emphasizes praxis in terms of Kanaka Maoli assertions of self-determination, and to move beyond the legal apparatus of recognition, while Coulthard challenges liberal pluralism and the assumption that colonial devastation and contemporary differences between the state and Indigenous peoples can be reconciled through a process of recognition. As an alternative, he also turns to praxis by highlighting the process of revaluing, reconstructing, and redeploying Indigenous cultural practices based on self-determination. Audra Simpson's work is also instructive here. In *Mohawk Interruptus*, she combines political theory with ethnographic research among the Mohawks of Kahnawake in southwestern Quebec to examine their struggles to articulate and maintain political sovereignty through centuries of settler colonialism by insisting on the integrity of Haudenosaunee (Iroquois Confederacy) governance and refusing US and Canadian citizenship. Simpson theorizes what she terms a politics of refusal in sharp contrast to the politics of cultural recognition and argues that one sovereign political order can exist nested within a sovereign state, despite tensions regarding jurisdiction and legitimacy.

In the contemporary Hawaiʻi context, there are two prevailing nationalist projects—one for federal recognition of a native governing entity within the US state, and the other for international recognition of an independent state. My book,

Paradoxes of Hawaiian Sovereignty, reveals the shortcomings of both. Since they insufficiently deal with the particularities of the Hawaiian case, in light of a long legacy of colonial bio-politics under the kingdom, along with US occupation and settler colonialism, neither federal law nor international law fully reckons with these historical injustices. The proposed tribal model for Hawaiians is a *federally driven* solution to the so-called Hawaiian problem—an attempt to extinguish the Hawaiian question as a moral, political, and legal one. Despite attempts by state officials to contain the outstanding Hawaiian sovereignty claim within US federal policy, the claim to Hawaiian independence endures and is still playing out. Yet there is a paradox of Hawaiian sovereignty; Kanaka Maoli have an extinguished claim to independent nationhood, but it hinges on the very things that degraded the Indigenous polity in the early to late nineteenth century, and now works to discount that social position today. And yet, the US government—if ever pressed by the world community—cannot substantiate its claim to the Hawaiian Islands since the archipelago was never ceded through treaty or conquest. Even the US government acknowledged this in its 1993 apology to the Hawaiian people.

The Hawaiian situation demands an approach that is not state-centered (US or otherwise) in order to fully explore recuperating a decolonial modality. There are rich examples in Hawai'i that offer ethical projects centered on non-exploitative forms of sustainability and well being for the *lāhui*, the Hawaiian people/nation, a definition not dependent on any state formation. These are grounded in non-statist forms of Indigenous Hawaiian sovereignty, what we might refer to today as *ea*, the power and life force of interconnectedness between deities, ancestral forces, humans, and other animals, and all elements of the natural world. Kanaka Maoli need not rely on the US state and its subsidiary (the 50th state of the "union") nor for the resurrection of the Hawaiian kingdom. Given the complex political realities Kanaka Maoli face in the form of aggressive attacks on the Hawaiian nation and its lands, pursuing *ea* is critical. Hence, increasingly, Kanaka are laboring to revive and strengthen Hawaiian cultural practices.

How do you think indigenism and anarchism are related to feminism and queer politics and activism?

I think it depends on the context in terms of cultural specifics. In general, anarchism and feminism are linked in terms of commitment to overturning domination, and feminism tackles that in the realm of gender and related realms. I understand that which is queer to be non-normative and not about sexual orientation per se, even though people often use it as an umbrella term to include LGBT individuals.

I started to identify as both feminist and queer at the same time I found my way to anarchism, which also was when I started to identify with Hawaiian projects for sovereignty, land, and self-determination—and began to identify as an Indigenous nationalist. As I became more involved in the Hawaiian movement, I found that feminist assertions within the Hawaiian nationalist movement were silenced (by men and women activists alike)—but not because people were uninterested in gendered forms of empowerment. I think it is because they see feminism as redundant to gendered decolonization. I have found that the notion of Indigenous Hawaiian feminism is not seen as irreconcilable with Hawaiian cultural norms or "tradition"; instead, it is typically viewed as unnecessary and superfluous since many Kanaka Maoli regard patriarchal norms as a colonial import. This popular understanding is critical to the current nationalist context, where the movement as a whole encourages a rethinking of the Hawaiian past as a basis for cultural reclamation projects in the service of political mobilization.

Lately I have been thinking a great deal about the ways in which people who have anarchist sensibilities may not explicitly identify as "anarchist"—and how many times this distancing from the label is understood as somewhat irrelevant in cases where there is still an expressed affinity for principles traditionally associated with anarchist organizing. Some might see the question of women disassociating from the label "feminist" as an analogue—and that it does not matter (or should not matter) so long as the grounding principles are being engaged (e.g. a commitment to gender equity and liberation). But I am not so sure. I think there may be something more going on that is epistemological, that it may be about meaningful difference, even if there seem to be resemblances on the face of it.

In another book project I have been working on, *Decolonizing Traditions: Native Hawaiian Women and the Politics of Feminism*, my work investigates how feminism may pose an epistemological problem for Hawaiian sovereignty and the reclamation of *mana wahine* (women's power) given the fact that feminism has its very origins in the Western rights discourse of liberal humanism and is fundamentally about equality and the shift away from tradition in order to confer rights. While there is no problem with that political project in itself, Indigenous Hawaiian women have identified Indigenous traditional models of liberation that draw on a radical difference from Western societies.

I think about this in relation to sexuality as well. The precolonial Hawaiian world, which is well documented given that we are talking about a period up to the late eighteenth century, allowed for same-sex sexual expression, polyandry, and polygyny. So, when I think about what constitutes "queer" when same-sex sexuality was part of Indigenous customary practice, it feels odd referring to it as non-normative in the contemporary period. Marriage was introduced by Calvinist missionaries from New England in the early nineteenth century, and with marriage came coverture—the subordination of women's civil status. This is not to romanticize precolonial Hawaiian society, which had a very stratified and hierarchical kinship system. Women and men were positioned in relationship to each other in an egalitarian way, but with the qualifier—in relation to each other within their respective genealogical rankings. And, of course, there will always be debates about what constitutes "tradition" when engaging in projects of Indigenous resurgence.

You taught a class on "Anarchy in America: From Haymarket to Occupy Wall Street." What did you get from this experience?

I teach this class semi-regularly. So far, it is one of my favorite courses. The class has three parts: histories; philosophies and theories; and activism. Each time I teach it I revise the syllabus to respond to student input and also to keep up with new literature in the fiend of anarchist studies. And in terms of teaching, I get to stay on top of the new literature in anarchist studies, and read in areas I might not otherwise, while also thinking about the contemporary political moment in critical ways. I aim to introduce students to select aspects of anarchist political thought and praxis in the United States and the ways that anarchism has been represented positively, vilified, or dismissed. Anarchism as a political philosophy and practice is an important, but little known, aspect of American culture and society. For most of the students who have been in the class so far, it is their first introduction to anarchism.

We also engage critical approaches to anarchism with a focus on the US state, examining how different peoples have a different relationship to that state structured by settler colonialism, slavery, and white supremacy. For example, we look at the ways in which the American individualist libertarian tradition draws on a white nativist cadre of thinkers who appropriated indigeneity for themselves—whether we are talking about the "Founding Fathers" or the transcendentalists.

The course also offers room for students to research their own topics of interest; the final project is a political pamphlet that is a cross between a research paper and a manifesto. They develop their own relationship to the different sets of debates and social problems and figure out their own respective investments. The range of topics they come up with for their pamphlets are usually quite original and compelling. It is also meaningful for me to learn from the students, through their insights and personal growth in terms of ethical orientations regarding both politics and intellectual development.

In February 2014, you launched a radio program called "Anarchy on Air" (broadcast through WESU) with a group of students. Why was this project meaningful for you? What is its genealogy?

The radio program, "Anarchy on Air" emerged from the "Anarchy in America," course, but it has an earlier antecedent. The first anarchist radio program I co-hosted and co-produced through WESU with a group of Wesleyan students was called "Horizontal Power Hour." That show was inspired by my attendance at the inaugural meeting of the North American Anarchist Studies Network, which was held in Hartford in October 2009. Shortly after, I recruited a dozen students and we debuted the show in September 2010. The program ran through May 2010, and all 59 episodes are archived online: https://horizontalpowerhour.wordpress.com/. Eventually, most of the students graduated and we did not replenish the working group. In the meantime, I taught the "Anarchy in America" course for the first time, and one of the students who had been very active in producing "Horizontal Power Hour" enrolled in it (she was the last student from the earlier show who was still on campus). After the class ended, she and I brainstormed reviving an anarchist radio show and recruited people from the class. We decided to give it a different name, hence "Anarchy on Air." The program launched in February 2014, and all of our audio archives can be accessed online: http://anarchyonairwesu.tumblr.com/.

This project has breathed new life into ways of being in the academy in general, and at Wesleyan University in particular.

What would you say to a non-Indigenous, settler anarchist living in America or in Europe, who would claim to be willing to help Indigenous movements and struggles?

I should add that I think any deep critique of state power, in keeping with my US and Canada examples, is to consider what a decolonial anarchist approach entails. For example, contemporary Canadian and US federal laws that govern Indigenous peoples continue to be grounded in the doctrine of discovery, which is rooted in fifteenth-century papal bulls. These mandates by pope established Christian dominion and subjugated non-Christian peoples by invalidating or ignoring aboriginal possession of land in favor of the government whose subjects explored and occupied a territory whose inhabitants were not subjects of a European Christian monarch.[2] That

---

2   See Steven Newcomb, *Pagans in the Promised Land: Decoding the Doctrine of Christian Discovery* (Golden: Fulcrum Publishing, 2008). He explains the Inter caetera ("Among other works") a papal bull issued by Pope Alexander VI on May 4,1493, which granted to Spain (the Crowns of Castile and Aragon) all lands to the "west and south" of a pole-to-pole line 100 leagues west and south of any of the islands of the Azores or the Cape Verde islands. Because there were differing interpretations, with some arguing that it was only meant to transform the possession and occupation of land into lawful sovereignty—and others, including the Spanish crown and the conquistadors, interpreting it in the

is why there is a widespread movement among Indigenous peoples to demand that the Vatican revoke the 1493 edict, especially since European and Euro-settler nations continue to use the doctrine to rationalize the conquest of Indigenous lands in order to perpetuate the legal fiction of land possession.

For instance, US federal Indian law and policy have long been premised on Old Testament narratives of the "chosen people" and the "Promised land," as exemplified in the 1823 Supreme Court ruling *Johnson v. McIntosh*, a landmark decision that held that private citizens could not purchase lands from Indian tribes. The foundations of the court's opinion lay in the "discovery doctrine." Based on this ruling, the US government still today considers tribal nations as mere occupants of their traditional homelands with "use rights" based on the court's invention of the concept of "aboriginal title."

As Murray Sinclair—Chair of Canada's Truth and Reconciliation Commission—asks, "What would be the basis for rationalizing Crown sovereignty if the Doctrine of Discovery is no longer available?"[3] This reminds me of Noam Chomsky's working definition of anarchism as "an expression of the idea that the burden of proof is always on those who argue that authority and domination are necessary."[4] If they

---

widest possible sense (e.g. that it gave Spain full political sovereignty), the following year the issue was clarified by the Treaty of Tordesillas (June 7, 1494). That agreement divided the newly discovered lands outside Europe between Portugal and the Crown of Castile, along a line of demarcation about halfway between the Cape Verde islands (already Portuguese) and the islands entered by Christopher Columbus on his first voyage (claimed for Castile and León).

3   See Chinta Puxley, "Vatican May Be Asked to Repeal Papal Bulls of Discovery on 'Heathen' Aboriginals," *The Canadian Press*, February 10, 2015, www.cbc.ca/news/aboriginal/vatican-may-be-asked-to-repeal-papal-bulls-of-discovery-on-heathen-aboriginals-1.2951620 (accessed January 19, 2016).

4   See "On Anarchism: Noam Chomsky Interviewed by Tom Lane," ZNet, December 23, 1996, https://chomsky.info/19961223/ (accessed January 19, 2016).

cannot, then "the institutions they defend should be considered illegitimate."

To get back to your question, I think the key to a non-Indigenous, settler anarchist willing to help Indigenous movements and struggles can start by learning more about the specific area(s) where they live and work—and to understand the history of the indigneous peoples whose territory or homeland they are on. I see that as a prerequisite for assessing what sorts of meaningful connections with the Indigenous people of that particular place might be forged, which is how one can come to understand what their priorities are in terms of building meaningful solidarity.

Therefore, I think whether they are living in the Americas or Europe makes a big difference in terms of what sort of solidarity one might engage in. For example, if a non-Indigenous person is living in the United States or Canada, the terms of engagement are necessarily different given that they are living on the land of an Indigenous people that has been claimed by the settler colonial state. So, there's an ethical question in terms of anarchist praxis—how to practice a commitment to eradicating domination while being structurally positioned as part of the settler colonial project?

One example is a non-anarchist, grassroots organization called Neighbors of the Onondaga Nation (NOON), based on Onondaga lands in what is known as Syracuse, New York. The group supports the sovereignty of the traditional government of the Onondaga nation, including its right to reclaim land. NOON also works to promote the understanding of and respect for the Onondaga people and culture within the broader Central New York community by working to educate themselves and others about the history of the relations between the US government, New Yorkers, and the Onondaga Nation.

In closing, I simply want to underscore that decolonization is imperative for everyone striving to live in a world without non-consensual domination, but the practice looks different for Indigenous people(s) and those who are living on lands they are not Indigenous to. But decolonization is a *practice*—application or use of an idea, belief, or method—as is anarchism. And it is crucial we bring them together.

The Pluto Press Newsletter

Hello friend of Pluto!

Want to stay on top of the best radical books
we publish?

Then sign up to be the first to hear about our
new books, as well as special events,
podcasts and videos.

You'll also get 50% off your first order with us
when you sign up.

Come and join us!

Go to bit.ly/PlutoNewsletter

Thanks to our Patreon subscriber:

Ciaran Kane

Who has shown generosity and
comradeship in support of our publishing.

Check out the other perks you get by subscribing
to our Patreon – visit patreon.com/plutopress.
Subscriptions start from £3 a month.

PGIL2023USA